MONEY $tories

Money $tories

How Money & Spirit Combine to Create Abundance

Connie Carmichael Hill

Gmknite Publishing
Portland, OR

Gmknite Publishing
PO Box 230461
Portland, OR 97281
gmknite@gmail.com
gmnite.com

Copyright 2013   Connie Carmichael Hill

All rights reserved. This book may not be reproduced in whole or in part, stored in a retrieval system, or transmitted in any form or by any means – electronic, mechanical, or other – without written permission from the publisher, except by a reviewer, who may quote brief passages in a review.

ISBN 978-0615761589

1. Wealth – Buddhism 2. Mindfulness
3. Finance – personal ethics 4. Spirituality

Cover photo credits: Connie Carmichael Hill

For my friend, Karen Schneider, who many years ago told me I should write a book of Connie Stories.

Contents

Acknowledgements	1
Introduction	3
1. My Path toward Abundance	7
Stories of Value	17
2. Jennifer Louden...The God-Shaped Hole	18
3. Hal Zina Bennett...About Value	26
4. Pam Oslie...Creating Our Own Reality	38
5. Amit Goswami...Quantum Prosperity	50
Stories of Trust	59
6. Tama Kieves...Following in the Steps of Marianne Williamson	60
7. James Wanless...Money in My Cards	70
8. Lewis Mehl-Madrona...Releasing Struggles	80
9. Maridel Bowes...Provision	88
Stories of Faith	101
10. Carol Redmond...Angel at My Door	102
11. Mark Dodich...Follow My Dream	110
12. Quirina Kryger...My Highest Good	122
13. Erin Donley...Moving toward My Truth	130
Stories about Dharma	143
14. Stan Madson...Right Livelihood	144
15. Lori Wilson...More than Just Affirmations	152
16. Jacqueline Mandell...Mindfulness of Money	162
17. Joanne McCall...Knowing What You Want	170
18. Peace Pilgrim...Pilgrimage for Peace	182
Closing	191

Acknowledgments

Thank you to all of my friends and family who have helped with this project, reading and giving insights and feedback and support: Sheila King, Sharlene Inglis, Para Winingham, Debby and John Wohlmut, Charlotte Blair, Cathy Breslaw, Diane Warren, Marty Anderson, Leslie Gorman, Karen Schneider, Hal Zina Bennett, Quirina Kryger, Debbie Geotz, Victoria Odde, Bill Gibert, my sisters, Carol Peoples and Jill Mitchell, my daughters, Kim and Jenna Hill, my mom, Mary Ellen Arment, my editors, Jill Kelly and Gigi Estabrook, Sage Waitts for cover assistance, and all of those interviewed for this book.

Introduction

Though I've struggled with money most of my life, I've also had a deep-down belief that if a person was in their right livelihood or expressed faith and/or trust or really knew spirit, God, or whatever their word for that being was, then their lives would almost miraculously fall into place and they would have what they needed. On the one hand, that belief feels like magical thinking. But on the other hand, I've seen it work.

A few years ago I went on a journey to "prove" this belief and that is what this book is about. Through 16 interviews about money and life, I've begun to see life in new and different ways.

What I found was that most of the people I interviewed didn't necessarily "know what they knew" until I asked them. All had a sense of spirituality, though they don't necessarily call it that. Some call it happiness, others see it as no longer worrying or letting go of resentment, or maybe their personal story.

About half of the people said that though having money was important, it was not at the top of their list of values. Some were comfortable with money and had a sense of trust that where they were led was where they needed to be and that the resources they needed were available to them.

Money Stories

Others struggled with money but came to a time when they had to make changes in their lives to stay on the path on which they wished to continue. But all have a sense of comfort with their resources and the path they are on. They know that despite struggles, they are taken care of and have what they need.

This Is Not a How-to-Book

This book is not meant to tell you how to think about money or that money must go with spirituality. It's an exploration of how money works for the people I interviewed here. I'm hoping it will be of service to you.

I met many of these people through my job as event coordinator at New Renaissance Bookshop in Portland, Oregon: scheduling authors and speakers was a big part of that job. I met Quirina Kryger when I lived at the beach and our friendship has continued. I met Mark Dodich through astrology before he was a full-time astrologer, and before I moved to the coast. Pam Oslie gave me and my youngest daughter readings over the years and helped guide us to bigger lives. Erin Donley and Carol Redmond were co-workers at the book store. And Peace Pilgrim's story has fascinated me for years. She took a different money path — the path of not using money at all and has become one of my most helpful teachers.

Before I got serious about interviewing these people, I practiced on my favorite cousin, Bill Gibert, when I was visiting him in San Francisco before he died. The spiritual part of money for Bill was what he could do with it: have a comfortable place to live, good food to eat, a good car to get around in, entertainment, and the ability to travel. Bill and I talked a lot about money and spirituality. I give him credit for the fact that this book got done at all.

Introduction

How to Use This Book
In the introduction of Hal Zina Bennett's book Write Starts, he talks about "making this book your own." Folding down the corners of favorite pages, writing in the margins, underlining sections, writing down passages from other resources on the field note pages in the back. He also says that his book is not necessarily to be read cover to cover, but might be a companion for inspiration. I hope that this book will be one of those companions that you keep by your bed or by your computer or carry with you for inspiration. I also love to see yellow stickies hanging out of well-loved books, marking places that are important to the reader. Many of my books are thus decorated.

At the end of each chapter you will find a ***Things to think about*** section that you can use to help you work with the information in each story. I have left blank pages at the end that you can make notes, answer the questions, or come up with questions of your own to help you look at your own money story.

The people interviewed here helped me learn about abundance. They each seemed to have their money acts together and they were willing to share their story. Each conversation was immensely meaningful, and I am honored that these generous women and men allowed me to exercise my curiosity and talk with them about this "forbidden" subject.

I learned a lot about myself through these conversations and I hope you will, too.

Chapter 1

My Path toward Abundance

"I began this project thinking only of money and spirituality, but I soon began to see that spirituality is different for each person. To me spirituality is not about the church a person goes to or their religious beliefs. It's about their sense of connection to something larger than themselves.
Connie Carmichael Hill

What if money ran the lives of everyone around you, but your focus was different? What if you wanted to do what you loved but were afraid you'd starve or end up pushing a shopping cart down the street? These were some of my thoughts when I first started toying with the idea of working for myself more than 20 years ago. What if I couldn't make it work?

Do What You Love and the Money Will Follow by Marsha Sinetar suggested that I could "make it" doing what I loved, but did it really work? Did the author have a secret to share? The answer was yes, it really did work, but a lot of other tasks needed to be done to make it work. It is necessary to hange our deeply held attitudes and beliefs. I still struggle with this at times. But I do believe that if you do the work, the money WILL follow. I also believe that it may be several steps forward and a couple back, before proceeding forward again.

Money Stories

My Money Story

When I was about 12, my family moved from one comfortable, well-known-to-me neighborhood to another that was unfamiliar and unknown. Maybe because of the move, I started looking around me and seeing money inequalities and wondering about them. I was the oldest sibling in a large family, and it seemed to me that we struggled to meet our needs, let alone our wants. Families of friends didn't seem to struggle as much. What was it they did or knew that we didn't? I'm still watching decades later to see if I can answer this question.

At 13, I began babysitting for neighboring families and loved the money that came with an evening's work. At 15, with a work permit in hand, I began earning 25 cents more an hour at the local dime store than I did babysitting and the hours were more regular. None of my friends had jobs until they were older, but I loved the new sense of freedom that having money brought.

Between 15 and 45, I worked many jobs for other people, thinking working for someone else was the only way to bring in the necessary income. But in my 40s, the need for more freedom, the wish to be my own boss, and the desire to do something that made me feel creative became more and more important.

Living close to the ocean had always been my dream. When I was 50 the Oregon coast started calling my name, and I went. Jobs were few and far between in Oregon coastal towns, so I reinvented myself as an astrologer, a coach, and a drum-making and drumming teacher. I also tele-commuted doing special projects for New Renaissance Bookshop in Portland.

My Path toward Abundance

Secrets

I struggled with money from the time I left home at 19 but I kept my money struggles secret for many years. Just before I started my first full-time job, my dad took me aside and told me I should never talk about money, especially not how much I made. Thanks to those words I kept a secret that led me to scarcity, overspending, low-paying jobs, a profusion of unpaid bills, lots of fear, and no understanding of abundance or manifesting. I didn't know what normal money behavior was for many years.

When my secret finally became a conversation, my life began to change and loads lifted off my shoulders. Money started to flow more easily. Sharing those secrets allowed me to see that I was not alone. Many people struggle with money, and most try to keep their struggles secret as well, out of shame and guilt. Voicing the struggles helped me to release a lot of shame.

For me, releasing scarcity and fear is an ongoing process, and hang-ups and beliefs learned years ago (many that I thought I'd released!) still occasionally show themselves. Whenever I get cocky and think I know it all, the flow slows! Then I learn another piece about humility and compassion, for myself and others.

Learning to Manifest

I can manifest money and other resources but not consistently. Even so, how money flows in my life is now my barometer. If money stops flowing, I'm usually fearful and worried, and there are things I need to look at. My fear is almost always about something other than money. I might be heading for life changes and the fear is popping out. Or I'm needing more creativity in my

Money Stories

life. I may be forgetting that abundance is much more than just money. There may be relationship lessons I needed to learn. All of these lessons are just part of my life's journey.

When I moved to the beach in 1995, I was able to manifest what I needed to pay my bills for four years, but every month or so I'd get anxious and worried and forget to trust. When I remembered to ask Spirit to fix it, peace would come, as well as what was needed, maybe not in bucket loads, but my needs were always met the entire time I lived at the coast. Trust and peace would come but after awhile I'd forget and have to go through the same process again. Consistency and trust are teaching me to look at more than just my bank account.

On My Path

My life path made a big transition about 20 years ago as a result of a vision quest. I had been laid off from my mainstream job and was working part-time cleaning houses and didn't know what my next step would be. Even though I was sure I couldn't afford it I signed up for the quest. Amazingly, once I registered, the money appeared.

Shortly after signing up I received a packet of information about things to bring and do before the vision quest. One item on the list to bring was a shield. I began to work on it right away. I "knew" my shield needed to be made of elk raw hide – the same skin I used to make drums – with willow branches around the edge. Then I needed to paint something on the face of it, but what?

First, I made a list of the animals I "wanted to go with me." Then, I began pulling cards from my Medicine Card Deck. None of the animals on my list came up. But my power animal, turtle, which I'd been work-

My Path toward Abundance

ing with for several years and was sure was no longer my animal, came up first. I had thought something really powerful like eagle or hawk would be necessary. But turtle wanted to come. So, turtle went in the middle with Native American power colors: yellow, red, black and white.

Next, I painted the earth and sky and the 28 moon phases. Then I attached feathers to the bottom of the shield.

I thought the shield was finished, but the Friday night before the quest, our leader, Marcy Calhoun, told us to put what we wanted to leave behind and/or to transform on the back of the shield. I drew pictures and put words to represent depression, anger, my divorce, dependence on others, my masks, judgments, and a path with question marks to represent finding my path.

The vision quest began early on Saturday. We met at a location north and west of Portland, up in the hills overlooking the Columbia River. The house had several acres of forested land around it.

We could bring tents, if we wished, and we came together for meals and talking circles several times during the quest. This was much easier than a typical vision quest, which takes you out on the land with no shelter, food, or communication with others for two or more days.

A few days before the quest, I kept getting a mental picture of what my quest space would look like. When I got to the location, I went right to a space at the edge of the woods and stopped. I tried to walk up into the woods, thinking that my space should be more hidden but then turned around and came back to the original spot. When I turned and looked out from where I was standing, it was the same view I'd had in my mind for a week.

Money Stories

At one of our meal gatherings, our leader asked us to think of a time in our lives and to visualize it as we did a guided meditation. Then we all talked about what came to us. Mine was when I was 5 and stayed overnight with my paternal grandmother. During our time together we made homemade noodles, which I still think of to this day as some of the best I've ever tasted. The most fun, though, was when my grandmother made me sugar and butter sandwiches and cut the crust off the bread. I still remember what a treat the sandwiches and the time alone with my grandmother were.

The weekend of our quest was stormy, cold, and awful, but I remember being cozy and warm in my tent, snuggled in a sleeping bag. We spent from sundown until the next morning alone in our campsites, and my night was amazing.

First, the quest leader came around as her alter ego, Coyote Woman, trying to lure us out of our spaces or to give us misinformation. After Marcy came by my space, I went to sleep and then woke up with a vision of my grandmother (who had died several years before) bringing me a plate of sugar and butter sandwiches to nourish me on the quest. She said it was time for me to take on the new name, Grandmother Knight. (A friend, who studies numerology, later told me that spelling the second word with a 'k' was much more powerful than without.)

That was more than 20 years ago and I'm still growing into that name.

Another awareness from the quest came at the end. On Saturday as I was setting up my camp, another quester came out of the woods and asked me if this was the path. I said "No, it was my camp." Later, while tearing down my camp, I realized that my camp was in the

My Path toward Abundance

middle of a path out of the woods. And I was suddenly aware that I was always on my path!

As I write this I realize that that weekend began a new path for me, one that was much more shamanic and symbolic, the one that involves drumming and drum making and astrology. It also involves being less traditional in the way I've lived and made money. It has not always been an easy path, but it has been one I've loved and one that fits me. It brought me to the path of writing this book.

Writing a Book

As I said before, for many years I've been curious about the way money works in people's lives. In 1997, the idea came to me that I should write about money and spirituality, and I wrote in fits and starts but it didn't seem to get anywhere and I really had no idea what this project was going to become. Then, several years later when I was about ready to give it all up all together, it came to me that I love hearing people's stories, so I began asking interesting people to tell me their money stories.

For as long as I can remember, I've loved to "see what makes people tick." Why do people do what they do, want what they want, pick what they pick, say what they say, and so on. So, the question "Why do people spend money the way they do and if a person has a spiritual side, does that change how money works for them?" became a natural extension of that. Hearing people's stories helps ME make sense of the world.

When I first began this project, I had to watch who I talked to about it. I was so vulnerable that any accidental unkind words would stop me for months. But the love of these stories would always pull me back.

Money Stories

I began this project thinking only of money and spirituality, but soon I began to see that spirituality is different for each person. To me, spirituality is not about a person's religious beliefs. It's about their sense of connection to something larger than themselves, such as creativity, right livelihood, prayer, meditation, or tarot.

Finding Abundance

Most of my life I've wished I had better control of money, wished I could manifest it more easily, wished I didn't struggle so much with it. To help me release those struggles I've tried counseling, 12-step work, being coached, affirmations, and working with the Law of Attraction. After all of these years, my money flow is still inconsistent. Working with these conversations has brought up many issues, but it has also allowed me to let go of more of my anxiety about money, about what is enough, and about scarcity. I've noticed many changes in my attitude toward money. These interviews have helped me let go of beliefs about being unworthy, that I'll never be secure, and that money has to come to us in only one way.

My biggest lesson is that my money story is up to me. The struggles can seem horrible and can keep me from living my life fully and well, or they can teach me about life and the choices I've made and lead me to perhaps make different choices in the future. Choosing to see the struggles simply as lessons has helped me open up to a more abundant life.

My Path toward Abundance

Things to think about:
What is your money story? Do you have secrets? Why have you kept these secrets? Has keeping these secrets helped you or hurt you? In your life, are there times when your path has taken new directions? Have these new forks in your path helped you stand in your power? What caused the forks and what do the new paths look like?

My path has taken several such turns. One was the vision quest and another was attending a 12-step group, which let me know that my secrets were keeping me from moving forward on my path. I took that first step to the 12-step group because of the pain I was feeling and within weeks my "secrets" were out in the open and could no longer keep me stuck.

Stories of Value

Money Stories

I first heard about **Jennifer Louden** in the early 1990s when a friend gave me a copy of *The Woman's Comfort Book* for a birthday present. I loved that book! I'd pull it out when I needed guidance. I especially like the chapters that call for hot baths and candles. Jennifer published several other comfort books over the next few years and then in 2007 she published *The Life Organizer* and I had the opportunity to host a book talk. I was excited to get the chance to meet Jennifer. She is so much fun to listen to. She had everyone in stitches one minute and then would throw out serious and wonderful gems. Her notion about stories is what gave me the idea for the title of this book. Thank you, Jennifer.

Chapter 2

The God-Shaped Hole

"What is finally enough for you is a great question to crack open your money story. So often our money story is linked to a sense of "If I can just get this, then I will have enough." As we know, that is a never-ending chase for "enough" that never arrives. I call it "filling the God-shaped hole." Jennifer Louden

Jennifer Louden has written six books on well-being and personal wisdom that have sold nearly 900,000 copies in 9 languages. Her books include her first, *The Woman's Comfort Book,* and her most recent, *The Life Organizer: A Woman's Guide to a Mindful Year*. Jennifer led her first women's wilderness retreat at age 29, gave birth at home, and has coached, as she says, a bazillion amazing people. She was able to "find the good" in three years of tragedy, including her husband's diagnosis of leukemia and losing a big contract as a national spokesperson on the same day that a dear friend died. Jennifer says she worked her butt off to get on *Oprah* and then realized, walking off the stage, that wasn't her real desire – a precious life lesson. She also walks around astonished by life most of the time! www.jenniferlouden.com

Let's talk about money. Tell me about money in your life and how it works for you or doesn't.

Money Stories

Until six or seven years ago, money was very important. It played a huge part in my being driven to be successful. It's the religion I was raised with, the religion of success through entrepreneurship. It was what my father loved more than anything, except us. Money is how he measured his success as a human being. He taught us the importance of being successful and measured success as a human being by making money.

I've never been much of a "stuff" person and have never liked to count my money or check my investments. My dad would do that every day. He'd watch the stock market and would know how much he was worth at the beginning and end of each day. He was so disappointed when I didn't know exactly how much my income and taxes were at any given time.

It was a positive influence in many ways, because I never relied on a man for money or felt that was the way it should be or that I couldn't take care of myself. So there are lots of positive parts to that philosophy, but as a younger person, it drove me too much. It was hard on my first marriage because my husband was not very successful at earning money until our last few years together.

How did you develop a spiritual practice?

It began when I was 12 and discovered my sister's copy of *Be Here Now* by Ram Dass. For me, it has to be about yoga and meditation. Yoga has been important for about 25 years, and for nearly 20 years I've used meditation to check in with my witness. That helps me notice and dissolve my sense of self. These two are a huge part of my daily life.

You said in the last 20-25 years these have been important. Has your sense of money changed during that time?

The God Shaped Hole

The biggest change around money was in learning to change my story, primarily through my ontological philosophy in coaching. That, plus therapy, were the biggest shifts for me. They shifted my story around my marriage and about how things should be. My spiritual practice has given me a sense of no matter what, everything is ok. There is no attachment to things any more.

When my daughter was little, we had some acquaintances who were into *Your Money or Your Life.* The guy was in my ex-husband's men's group and the woman was in my moms group. They turned their home, which was not in a good part of town, into a boarding house as part of their money work. I remember thinking at the time, I couldn't live like that because it was not beautiful. That has changed for me.

This sense of needing things to be a certain way was tied up with money, but that connection isn't there anymore. Now, if I lost everything and couldn't live in my pretty little house, would that attachment come back? I don't think so. I could live in a pretty single room! But I'm not sure if I could still feel the same without clean clothes. How far could I go and not feel compromised? I'm not sure.

What do you mean by *story* and what does that mean in your life?

What opened up so many possibilities in my life has been understanding that what I tell myself about something is almost always a set of interpretations and not "The Truth." Interpretations are the way our mind works. My interpretations may not change, but I can become aware, at any given moment, of what they are and if they serve me or not. My set of interpretations around money caused me a lot of suffering, specifically when it came to my first marriage and my sense of myself

Money Stories

as a successful writer. I wanted to be a *New York Times* best-selling author. Otherwise, I wouldn't be successful. Strangely enough, though, that notion of success wasn't linked to money. It was linked to popularity, almost like high school!

You're a coach. Do you work with clients around these issues?

At the moment I've let my clients go. But in my years of being a coach and working with people in retreat settings, yes, I have worked with clients about spirituality but not money. Money has never been a big part of my focus. My coaching work has always been about people's perceptions about how they could create a life they loved and the money was only important in a round-about way.

I never really thought about money's connection to spirituality until you asked me. It might be that it's just not that interesting to me. Our stories about how we take care of ourselves or how we create or don't create are so much more interesting than how we make money or don't. Maybe I'm not ready to deal with that part yet.

For some of the people I've interviewed, money is rolled up in having the life they want.

I've dealt with clients around the questions: "Do you want to make a change? What do you want to give up for the change? What is your debt level?"

I think of that as paying attention to what is and that our commitments show up in our actions. We can say that we are committed with our words, but our actions show our real commitments. Is it more important to have a latte every day than to save for your freedom from a job you hate? How much compassion and awareness can we bring to that notion?

The God Shaped Hole

I remember one client that I coached out of a very high-paying job and into her own successful business so she could cut her commute and be surrounded by beauty. She really struggled with some things like "But if I do this, then I can't buy the drapes for my house..."

That's a real level of development you have to move through. Not everyone has the practices or the support to move through that level of development to "Wow, it really doesn't matter if I have those particular drapes or not."

The problem becomes: "Once I have the drapes, then will I be able to quit the job?" or "If I have the job, will I be able to afford a vacation, too?"

Some people will keep going around and around on that. Or they'll get into debt because they have to have it all. It's the "American Dream Story," that everyone should have everything they want, all the time, and it's a lie. The only way to have everything is through debt. The idea of debt is a conversation that most people don't have with their friends.

Have you had this kind of conversation with your daughter?

When she was younger, I struggled a bit with her need to have everything. I tried to teach her that we have choices. You have to learn what you really want. You have to decide what your style is, what you really want and what's most important to you. That's something lots of people never figure out.

My family's ethos was that if somebody asked how much I made, I must be very honest and tell them. I love to have conversations about what I make. In my brain trust, five of us met virtually. One of the first things we did was reveal how much we grossed. One friend called it "peering beneath the kimono." It was so

Money Stories

empowering to reveal our income to each other. It made me see that if the others made $300,000 a year, I could make it, too.

One friend, who had been part of the group, made $68,000 in one month! His conversation with me was "if I can do it, you can, too." He's an executive coach and one of my stories is that you have to be willing to be an executive coach or work with businesses to make that much. But that's just a story.

I love the idea of story and what a person's story is. That's what these conversations are about. What are people's stories around money and spirituality? When I began this project, my idea of money and spirituality was that the two had a kind of fit.

To me, the single most powerful precept we have is how we learn to observe what our constructs of reality are. How do we learn to become compassionate about these ideas? How do we get out of the grip of what we think is true and into a more spacious way of thinking? **I love the idea of story. I've heard it from other spiritual teachers, but you say it in such an accessible way.**

It's a twisty thing. In the hands of some teachers and groups, it becomes a source of violence. For me what's important is spiritual freedom. When you are spiritually free, story becomes something you can see yourself doing and not get tangled in. It doesn't matter. If you want to put your energy toward having a house on the water and having as much money as Bill Gates so you can give it away, great! But it's a game and that's what's missing for me with some groups and teachers.

I'm looking at a bookmark on my desk from the Newfield Network. The first question on the bookmark is "What is finally enough for you?" To me the connection between story and enough is really intimately connected.

The God Shaped Hole

In my book, *The Life Organizer,* part of my goal is to offer questions that crack open your story in different areas of your life. "What is finally enough for you" is a great question to crack open your money story. So often our money story is linked to a sense of "If I can just get this, then I will have enough." As we know, that is a never-ending chase for "enough" that never arrives. I call it "filling the God-shaped hole."

Things to think about:
What is "your story" around money? In other words, what do you tell yourself about the money in your life? Is it hard to draw money in? Are you doomed to struggle with money? Is the amount of money you make in the control of your boss or the company you work for? My money story for a long time was that I'd never have enough. Now I realize that "not enough" is a story I tell myself. I'm in control of my money, and trust and responsibility are much more important concepts to add to my story instead of whether I have enough or not. If having enough is my total focus, can I really ever have enough? Will there always be a longing for more?

Sit quietly and ask the question in your head or out loud, "What is my money story and what do I long for?" Then, listen to what thoughts jump in to your head. Just listen for a few minutes and see what comes. Write these thoughts down. Don't worry about whether you made them up or whether they are real or not. I find that if I listen and allow, the first thoughts that come to mind when I do this exercise are always right on. I just have to get my ego out of the way and keep it from questioning and berating and judging the important thoughts.

Money Stories

The book *Zuni Fetishes* by **Hal Zina Bennett** was my first introduction to Hal. I was trying to figure out what the various fetish animal symbols meant and his book fell on me at the store where I bought many carved animals. I LOVED this book! It helped me learn more about the animal energies and how to use them.

In about 1999 I was at the International New Age Trade Show and Hal was signing his newest book, *Spirit Circles*. I took up way more than my share of time in line talking with Hal and afterwards we kept running into each other around the show.

The final day of the show we were sitting and talking in a rest area and Hal mentioned that he had a small publishing company and that he did talks and workshops. I asked if he ever did talks or workshops about publishing. He said he hadn't but would think about it. Within a year Hal was up in Portland doing the first of many publishing and self-publishing workshops at New Renaissance Bookshop, and I attended every one! And Hal's encouragement is a big reason this book has been published!

Chapter 3

About Value

"What does money really mean? If we are on a spiritual path, is the way we are handling our money, and our relationships with others concerning money, in harmony with our own belief system? If not, what changes do we need to make to be congruent?" Hal Zina Bennett

Hal Zina Bennett's highly acclaimed work includes countless articles and more than 30 successful books, including *Spirit Circles, Write from the Heart, Zuni Fetishes,* and *The Well Body Book*. Hal's interest in creativity, human consciousness, metaphysics, and the ancient wisdom traditions began as a teenager, following a coma and a near-death experience that left him temporarily blind, during which time he was initiated into the reality of the inner world. Studies in ancient spiritual traditions over the next 20 years helped him to validate insights he'd had during his encounters with his own death and his visions of the world beyond. In addition to being a prolific author, Hal has helped over 200 authors develop their own work, several of them bestsellers.
www.halzinabennettcom

Money Stories

Can you tell me how money works in your life.

I'm concerned with "value for value" in all human exchanges. If you hire me to edit your book, I want to be able to deliver something that has real value to you. We honor each other's energy and skill. With the present corporate model, the bottom line is the bottom line. I have nothing against money. A currency system can still represent an exchange of human energy, a way of "storing" energy; that is the real bottom line.

For example, I occasionally teach shamanic workshops. People who are purists say that you don't take money for work that has a spiritual component. But what would they give in exchange? Paying money is the way this culture works. A dollar bill is a way of storing energy. It's a trade. I give you information and you give me dollars, and I can buy food and pay rent. This exchange allows me to do my work in the world. It's no different than giving me corn or a chicken barter. Coins, dollar bills, credit cards—these are just the way we have decided to do this exchange in our culture.

A number of years ago I ran a county day care center for social services. Exchanges as part of the tuition were one of the payment options. Some people would volunteer their time: giving of themselves in this way was incredibly generous. Others would bring in things like the cardboard cores from toilet paper rolls and egg cartons for art work and they'd think that was a good trade. It was true we used the articles they brought for making art with the children. But these people (who donated their trash) were unbelievable self-righteous about it. Yes, they were giving something, but giving something that they themselves didn't value or want. The not-so-hidden message was that they had very little respect for what we did at the center.

About Value

What is the difference between people who give of themselves and the ones who don't?

For me it's found in the principle of equal exchange. The universe runs on it. Whether the exchange comes as money or a trade, it has to be value for value. Value received for value given. Let me give you an example from my own life:

In my consulting work I only take on projects where I can give real value. People will come to me with a project that could take hours and days of my work and they might not get the value they want for the amount of work needed. My final charges would be many thousands of dollars and when I look at their project I see that they could never earn anywhere near that value back, neither in dollars nor in personal satisfaction.

To me this whole thing about money comes down to how much do we need to run the world, to eradicate poverty and conflict. We seem so far away from our primary source with money, so isolated from what we really require for health and happiness. What do we each need? We need protection from the weather, a place to live, food, friends, health care, clothing, a bit of savings and a few other things. We don't need this perverted idea corporate America has sold us that we always need more and more and more.

I look at what has happened in the area of publishing. It looks like people who have money to put behind their books can get them published. Do you feel that big book sellers have all the power to limit books that can become popular?

It's gotten incredibly challenging for authors. There is no mid-list (non-bestselling books) any more. In some ways, the digital revolution – print-on-demand publishing and e-Books – has democratized publishing. It makes it possible to publish a book for very little money up-front, putting that aspect of writing into the hands of the author. And that's good, for the most part.

But the rich still do get richer and publishing companies are sending lots of jobs to other countries. I live in a rural community where the unemployment rate is high. One day this man came around and introduced himself. He told me, look, I'm an alcoholic, but I can do this and that kind of work and if you give me a job to do, I'll finish it. He knew his limits and he put them right out front.

I hired him. He's a good worker within the limits he set down. Working with him helped me to understand that you can't always judge another person's value by your own standards. He's screwed up, but our relationship has been good and he's done good work for me, and he has earned some money. I've given him books to read since he showed an interest in my writing.

Very few people have respected him in this way. We have an exchange of energy: my money for the work he does. He can go buy food and live, and he doesn't become a burden to society, except occasionally when he gets thrown in jail for being drunk. But he's up front about it.

It's the bigger picture of what the man is about. Like the homeless situation, some who are homeless are pretty rotten people and hurt others. Many are down on their luck.

I know a man who is now retired. His job, before retirement, was to go around and buy up little companies. The mother company he worked for would use the little companies for tax purposes. They would milk these little companies dry and then dump them, then take tax breaks from the loss. Some of the companies they did this with were second- and third-generation

About Value

family-owned businesses. The man I'm talking about admitted to me that sometimes families were destroyed in the process. He even told about how several people had committed suicide. I asked him "Doesn't this bother you?"

His reply was, no, it didn't bother him. It was business, all just the bottom line. Meanwhile, he retired with a golden parachute and today is worth many millions. I've always wondered how people can live their lives like that. How can they compartmentalize their lives so profoundly? How many people are ruined by that kind of attitude? How many wars are fought as a result? My friend says it doesn't bother him that he was part of this kind of business. But it's got to damn well injure him at a deep and unconscious level. Ironically, he boasts of being "a good Christian," serves on church committees and is active in his community association. How does one live with such contradictions?

The idea that money can get to a place so far away from being sacred energy and dharma is scary to me. I believe that if you have the tenacity to stick to it you do get support from the universe. Energy does come around if you learn how to draw it in. But our culture does not teach us how to do this, at least not in a spiritual way where everyone benefits. And, I confess, I'm struggling with it myself.

I know a lot of spiritual teachers who can't do it either. They struggle with the notion of prosperity. I believe that we can be supported, but I don't have a formula for making it happen. Do you?

I don't either. Maybe it's important to simply be asking questions about how to do it, as you are doing in this book and in these interviews. I'm really grateful that you are doing this book, because it's one of the

Money Stories

things that needs to be clarified. How many people have you heard say, "I'm not in it for the money." But in a very real way we can't help but be into it for the money. It's how we define and exchange human energy.

I think the answer is that when you value what is important to you, you can see yourself as part of a bigger whole. Doesn't it ultimately come down to our relationship with the earth and each other? It really is Mother Earth. If we don't give energy back, we are harming the Mother and thus each other.

I just saw a cartoon with a turtle floating through the sky. On the turtle's back is a whole village of monkeys mining the shell of the turtle. The turtle is just swimming through space. You finally see one person who has communicated with the turtle and is trying to tell the community that they are hurting her. In the last scene she is diving into nothingness. Yes, this is what some native peoples call "Turtle Island," that is, Mother Earth. It's what we are doing to our planet and it really scares me. It is scaring everyone.

People around the globe hate us Americans for good reason. Corporate America says the bottom line is all there is. How did we ever come to that? To me money is sacred. When you have given your energy in trade for your money, your energy goes full circle.

Like my consulting work. It's easy for me to see on a day-to-day basis that my energy drops when I'm in a situation where I don't feel I can give a good return, a good value for my efforts. On the other hand I worked recently with a person, ghostwriting for her, and my work totaled over $35,000. During the process I asked her "What happens if you don't make this money back on the book? Not many books do that well."

About Value

She told me, "It was not about the money. I have the money to do this and in the meantime, you have no idea how important this is to me. It's not only the finished product I'm interested in; it's also about the process of clarifying and expressing something that is profoundly important to me."

Is her book about spirituality?

It's actually a business book based on spiritual principles and written as a novel. So the value here has to do with what's coming back to the other person. (I should add here that the book did end up doing very well and selling over 100,000 copies, so financially it worked out well for her.) I'm not always in a position to judge that. I can ask them if they are sure they are getting value out of the process. That's my responsibility to ask, not just do the work. Plenty of editors do this kind of work and will charge someone $50,000 to edit a book. They may never ask but, that exchange of energy is essential and pretty rare today.

To me the key is for people to pay attention and for us to open up a dialogue, to ask questions that keep us seeking new answers. What does money really mean? If we are on a spiritual path, is the way we are handling our money, and our relationships with others concerning money, in harmony with our own belief system? If not, what changes do we need to make to be congruent?

I think of people who are working in a corporate office. Maybe IBM and they experience a lot of contradiction. I used to work on training manuals for a friend. She was an organizational consultant and she wanted to write a book praising the company's CEO. This was to be a book about someone who was really endangering the planet and had done huge amounts of damage culturally, and in many other ways continued to do damage. I told her, "I respect you and I like working with you, but I cannot help you with this project."

She said, "You don't understand. This man's mission is to help feed the world."

I didn't buy it. "Go to the internet," I said. "His company has 10,000 law suits against it for environmental crimes. That's why I can't work with you on this book, not for any amount of money."

No, I didn't work with her and I was sad about losing her friendship. Six months later the whole thing blew up in her face and she suddenly saw what he had been doing and how, essentially, she had allowed herself to be blinded by his company's propaganda. On the other hand, she was working with upper management and maybe, in the long run, she will prove to have been part of an important healing process. As for me, there was no way I could have supported what that company was and is doing to the planet and to all of us who live here. Oh, yeah, the name of the company? Monsanto.

How did you come to the concept of value for value?

For me, when I started studying earth-based spiritual systems that was the part that brought so much into focus for me. The bottom line was that you need food and shelter and a harmonious relationship with Spirit, Source, or God…whatever name you give to the power greater than ourselves. It's really easy to see the core values through that lens.

I was a teacher for a long time. My first teaching jobs were with inner city, fourth-generation, welfare kids. We teachers would take them out into the country. Most had never been out of their neighborhoods.

About Value

We'd take them to farms in Petaluma and it was amazing; the kids didn't know that milk came from a cow or that eggs came from a chicken. We'd tell them and they'd say, "Eggs come out of the bootie of a chicken? Oh man, I'm never going to eat no more eggs!"

As a child it's not unusual to not know where our food comes from. But as an adult, we know milk comes from cows. Are we willing to kill a cow for its meat? Or chop the head off a chicken to eat chicken? My formula is if you can't kill it, then don't eat it. All living beings have some sort of consciousness, even a tomato or leaf of cabbage, so these choices are not easy.

I was a hunter as a kid. I know the consequences of killing an animal. It was heart breaking for me to hunt, though I did and it brought food to our table. Many sportsmen get such an adrenalin high, and almost go crazy with a sense of power when they kill something. They don't know how to deal with it, emotionally or spiritually. It is no wonder that they should also be confused about the value of money.

There is a story about Zuni hunters. They would first pray to the spirit of the animal they were going after, and pray that its passage into the other world would be easy, that its family would do well after its departure. You couldn't eat the meat unless you did all of these things and while the animal was taking his last breath you would rush up and exchange last breaths with him. That was the sacred way of hunting. Very few people would eat meat if they had to do all of that. And by extension, very few of us would touch money if we knew what was behind it, what companies, products and motives were somehow mixed in with it. To speak metaphorically, we would certainly not want to exchange

Money Stories

breaths with it, knowing what our money gets involved with, how it is used, what and who it eats in this day and age.

Things to think about:
What is your bottom line about money? What do you need to be comfortable? Do you need more or less than what is coming to you right now? How could you make this new bottom line happen? Is there anything you no longer need? Make a list of what you think you need to be comfortable, and what is no longer needed. I find often that clearing out what I no longer need opens a space to increase my flow. It may also take me in new directions such as that I need much less than I think or of looking at how wisely I spend the money that comes to me.

Money Stories

Pam Oslie and I have met in person only once, but I have known her for more than 20 years through phone readings. She was the first reader to tell me that I would write. In a reading she said that at first I wouldn't even realize I was writing. For years I put together the quarterly New Renaissance Bookshop newsletter, and I wrote and edited 18-32 pages of event and product information without realizing I was writing. After several years in that job, it hit me that I needed to write a book.

Since Pam was so instrumental in pointing me in that direction, I knew that hers needed to be one of these stories. Pam's aura color information has allowed me to step out and balance the energy of my violet (intuitive, adventurous, creative, freedom-loving) and green (idea-focused, disciplined,and rule-oriented) without one taking over. Both are necessary, according to Pam. Thank you, Pam, for your story.

Chapter 4

Creating Our Own Reality

"I think it's interesting that our constitution is founded on the fact that we have the rights to life, liberty, and the pursuit of happiness. Not happiness, but the "pursuit" of happiness. In this country we seem to have created this energy of pursuing happiness and never attaining it." Pam Oslie

Pamala Oslie sees auras and has discovered that different aura colors reveal specific personality types. She can help you learn how to identify your own aura colors, and then understand what they reveal about you. Pam is the author of three books, including *Life Colors* and *Love Colors*. She is a popular guest on hundreds of TV and radio shows, and in print media. Pam is professional, entertaining, and a crowd pleaser. Terry James of the Lex and Terry Radio Network says, "Pam is an amazing guest who made our phones ring non-stop (even after she was long gone)." www.auracolors.com

Tell me how money and spirituality work in your life.
They're not disconnected for me. Everything is energy and consciousness, including money. This particular energy shows up as money in my life because of my beliefs. If my belief is that I can make only "x"

Money Stories

number of dollars, but not more, that's what will show up.

My favorite meditation exercise is to visualize money floating down around me and landing in big piles. Every time I do that exercise, cash shows up in my life. Once, a man I'd never met found my book, read it; and sent me 100,000 shares of his company's stock. The company was brand-new but later the shares ended up being worth $10,000. So I received $10,000 from a complete stranger!

I told some friends who were really hurting for money about the exercise, and they did it every night for five or ten minutes. They'd sit in their bed and visualize money floating down around them. A few weeks later the wife got called by a game show (she loved game shows) and won $25,000 in one hour. They were amazed how well and how quickly it worked.

This exercise allows me to release the belief that by having money I'm taking it away from others. The energy shows up out of the ether, out of the sky, and takes whatever form I need.

What a great exercise! Where did you find it?

I usually get my inspirations from the Seth books. Those writings are my favorite. They taught me about energy and how to create what I desire to have in my life. As an example, one day I was wishing for more money so I could travel. After reading one of the Seth books, I realized it wasn't the money I wanted, it was actually the travel. I told myself, "Just see yourself traveling." And within a few days three people had called, one from Hawaii, one from Oregon, one from Florida, all saying "If I paid for your flight, would you come visit?" All of a sudden I had three trips. Cool!

Creating Our Own Reality

Just before you called, I was cleaning my house and thinking about the stuff I have. My house is really, really clean. Everything is white, with plants everywhere and I don't like clutter, but there was so much clutter.

My next thought was "Wait a second. Let's change that thought from the negative connotation of "clutter" to a more positive connotation of "abundance." You've created a lot of abundance in your life. That's what you've been asking for, abundance, and this is the form it has taken!"

As I said before, money is energy. It's not negative or the root of all evil; it's just energy taking the form of money. When we were little most of us were told money was dirty: "Don't put that in your mouth, it's dirty," If that was true for you, then from now on when it becomes an issue for you, pull out your money and pet it, like you would a little dog or cat, or treat it like you do those things you love. Treat it with the same kind and loving consciousness you would that animal or plant you love, and it's going to want to come to you. I encourage people to think those thoughts, and it works.

How interesting! I need to try that. Does it work with big issues?

Money is illusive if we have issues with it. If we imagine we have struggles with it, we do. Einstein said, "Imagination is more important than knowledge" because what we think we know can limit us. We've all been raised with the American ethic, which tells us we must work hard. I was told "If you don't do it, it won't get done," and "You can't have fun until your work gets done." But I've noticed my work never gets done! So, to me it's all about belief.

Money Stories

I have a friend who works and works and works, and she always has just enough money to get by, never more than she needs, never less. It's always exactly the amount she needs to survive. That is so bizarre to me. It's all about her beliefs about receiving. She draws a line on how much abundance or wealth or money she can have in her life.

It's about how willing we are to receive, not about how much we deserve. We all deserve abundance, but our issues are about allowing and accepting. The universe is infinite and it is infinitely abundant.

Think about "empty" space. Even the quantum physicists are now saying that there is not any empty space, even a vacuum is not empty. They used to say a vacuum was empty, but now if they suck everything out and then try to put something in the vacuum, they can't because that so-called empty space is teaming with energy.

I see the universe as infinite and infinitely abundant. So how much of that are you going to make use of in your life?

What do you say now to people who are really having problems with money?

I don't believe in victim or scarcity consciousness. It is my opinion that whatever we believe is what we create. Our beliefs and our thoughts create our reality.

Some ask, "If our beliefs create reality, why would some people believe in and choose to live in poverty places like Africa?" We don't know why souls choose what they do, but I believe they have their reasons. Sometimes you can actually see more peace and joy in their eyes than you see in the eyes of many people in the wealthier countries.

Creating Our Own Reality

Our constitution is founded on the fact that we have the rights to life, liberty, and the pursuit of happiness. Not happiness, but the "pursuit" of happiness. In this country we seem to have created this energy of pursuing happiness and never attaining it.

For people who are having a rough time, I encourage them to look at where they've placed their sense of security. Is it in their jobs, their pay check, their houses or cars? Some people say, "I have the security of a job. Someone pays me to work." But if the job suddenly ends, do they still feel secure? Do they know who they are? What do you believe about the universe? What do you believe about who you are and how you create? I see a lot of wake-up calls happening right now.

I have a lot of compassion, and I also trust that our souls know what they are doing. I can have compassion and also trust that people are either working something out or are getting a wake-up call so their souls can grow and evolve. Maybe their souls don't want to leave this planet saying, "Well, I had a job and money and I bought a house and then I died." A lot of people are becoming conscious right now and realizing what is really important.

I've been working on this book for a number of years and recently have thought that I shouldn't try to publish it right now because so many people are struggling. But at the same time, it feel like this is the perfect time to do this project.

Yes! For several reasons. You never have to hold back because people don't have money. There are always people who flourish, no matter the circumstances or the economy. And there are people who, no matter what the economy is doing, will still struggle. It's about our beliefs and that we create our own reality. There are people who think that's harsh, that it translates into me

Money Stories

blaming others for their problems. That's not it at all. It's about realizing that we have the power to create our lives and not be victims. Also, I think there is a lot more value in being an example of living abundantly than in there is in being poor.

Some people say, "If you know all of this and we create our own reality, then everything for you is perfect." But we are adventurous souls and create challenges for ourselves, mostly to see who we really are. Otherwise life would be boring or flat.

Words like *positive* and *negative* are useless; instead we all carry some elements of abundance and scarcity in us, and that's the point. The more we see who we are, the less we have to fear.

Any time fear comes up for me it's because I have forgotten the magnificent essence of who I am. Life is a big adventure and it's not about the outside circumstances. Many of us try to change things from the outside. Think of the analogy of watching a movie you don't like. We want to change what's on the screen instead of going back to the projector and changing the film that's going into the projector. I choose to believe that we create our own reality. Some people don't feel that way and that's fine with me.

Have you had times when you have struggled?

Sure. Even financially. I remember being a car hop at an A-&-W, making about $10 a shift. And growing up we were really poor. But it didn't seem to bother me much. Now I've created wealth and abundance in my life. To me wealth equates to freedom and joy.

But my growth and learning comes in the area of relationship struggles. My issue used to be wanting someone to love me. And in living with these struggles I came to the realization that this was really about how

Creating Our Own Reality

I was treating myself – the lack of love I had for myself. Now, I don't feel a lack of love. I love everyone and I'm happy where I am.

Wanting something predisposes a belief in lack. We're playing in the proverbial sandbox. It's not for me to judge whether someone else's experience in the sandbox is good or bad. We're here to have experiences, to learn, and to feel emotions.

There are certain emotions I don't prefer, so I don't choose them. If my thoughts bring me anxiety or worry or fear, I just choose something else. I'm so fascinated by life. We have thoughts and feelings and are alive. The idea of life to me is just wondrous. "Look, guys, we can think! We can feel things. It's so fabulous."

Of course, I also create days that are not my favorite, but then there's tomorrow!

You said you grew up in poverty, but that it never really bothered you. Can you tell me more about that?

As a youngster, you never really know that it's poverty. I look back and see my single mother raising four kids on $400 a month. We were really poor and ate a lot of canned soup.

When did you realize that you could change that picture?

I've been spiritual my whole life and wanted to follow Christ's example. You know the wedding feast where Jesus changed water into wine? Can't you just imagine people saying "Oh, my gosh, we've got a wedding feast and we're out of wine. We've got to get some money together and send somebody out to get more. We've got to get to the store right away. And we've got to work really hard." But Christ had no problem. Zip, and the water was changed to wine. I want to manifest at that level, so there's no struggle or racing around.

Money Stories

My money process started with Napoleon Hill's book *Think and Grow Rich*. I also studied Terry Cole Whitaker, Deepak Chopra, Richard Bach, Abraham, and a lot of other metaphysical teachers, but the Seth materials are my favorite teachers. Everything else has branched from those, and *Think and Grow Rich* began my transformation.

I'm reading *Seth Speaks* again. Each time I read it, I know "that" book didn't say that the last time. The publisher says the same thing: "These books are living and breathing and consciousness and keep changing." **I find the same thing with books that are really meaningful for me. I can read them one time and they are at one level and another time they say something totally different.**

They have a consciousness to them. We all use different carrots to motivate us. For some people the motivation is "I want to have love," so they work with that. For other people, what's important is health or money and abundance or being able to travel. We all use different carrots to help us grow and evolve.

Don't get me wrong. I do run into challenges with my own beliefs at times. It's like a riptide. Sometimes, I'm swimming and swimming and don't getting closer to the shore. I realize there is still a little belief underneath that is pulling me away from the shore.

This is the same reason some people didn't have success with the Law of Attraction and *The Secret*. They visualized what they wanted and didn't understand why it didn't manifest for them. They didn't realize they had countering beliefs that told them that money was bad or people wouldn't like them if they had money. So the reason they didn't get what they desired was they had fears pulling them back the other way.

Creating Our Own Reality

I think one of the reasons I'm working on this book is because negative beliefs about money and deserving have been my area of struggle. I've been working to release those beliefs much of my life. People come to me as an astrologer because they have the same struggles. I guess it's not a struggle; it's more the path I've come to walk and learn about.

There is right-livelihood. I love my work, but I also love walking on the beach. How can we make money doing that? I can work and work and money comes to me, but on days when I sit down and meditate and read my Seth books, things come to me so much more easily. And do I do that every day? No. My underlying belief is that if I don't work, it won't get done and everything will fall apart. Those beliefs are still ingrained in me!

I think one of the reasons things are falling apart around the planet right now is that our beliefs are being challenged. Recently, Swami Beyondananda was on my radio show. He said, "When a caterpillar starts to change into a butterfly, it literally falls apart." I love this part. "In the caterpillar's transformation it uses *imaginal* cells to achieve the change." That's what's going on right now out in the world. Everything is falling apart, the educational system, the medical system, housing and business. Everything is transforming like the caterpillar. I'm no longer interested in saving the caterpillar, I'm interested in helping the "butterfly of new consciousness" emerge.

People are beginning to realize you can't rely on job security or anyone else to make your lives feel secure. I don't believe it's the government's or anyone else's job to take care of us. It's our own opportunity to learn to create our lives. I don't want to get political, but in his first race, Obama said "Yes, WE can."

Money Stories

Everyone voted him in and then said "Now, President Obama, YOU go do it." Before the election, it was "we" not "you." We need to take responsibility for our lives

If there is something going on in my life, I need to change it from the inside. We are either creating or reacting. We can't do both at the same time. If you are spending time reacting and blaming, you're not putting your energy into creating. For me, life is fun and the universe is friendly. A lot of people who are scared and without money see the world as hostile and believe only the fittest survive. Actually, cooperation and connection are what's helped organisms survive and evolve.

Right now we are in the transition from the Piscean Age to the Aquarian Age. We are moving away from dualism toward unity. Does this have anything to do with your vision of what is happening?

My analogy is that we can't see because we are in the birth canal. We are birthing a new consciousness and becoming new beings. Birth pains and contractions are not that much fun. We get squeezed. We need to remember to breathe a lot, to relax and not go into fear. If we go into fear, we make the process a lot harder.

Those are a few of the traits of the Aquarian Age. It's away from duality, and toward the fact that we are all connected.

I just had someone on my show speak about near-death experiences. Everyone who has been on my show who's had a near-death experience is so awesome. They all say the same thing: that we are connected and are all one. We are not separate from each other. We are experimenting with creation. We can abdicate that ability and say we don't have any power and "everything out there is separate from us, and we don't have any control." That is the prevailing attitude right now.

I love quantum physicist Amit Goswami. He says people think reality is out there and finished, and

Creating Our Own Reality

we are separate from it and have nothing to do with it. But quantum physics says we change things by realizing our connection to it – that it radiates from us. We change things from the inside.

Don't get me wrong. I still create my own challenges and we all create challenges so we can experience and learn. I accept and trust that people's souls are creating experiences for a reason. They are choosing certain beliefs for their own growth and evolution. I strive to grow beyond rules, limitations, and "dogma." Did you know that dogma spelled backwards is "am god"?

Things to think about:
What do you define as your security? Is it your house or your job or your partner or something else? What would happen to you if you no longer had it? Would it destroy you or empower you to make changes? Are you in a place where you feel a lack of security? What can you do to make yourself feel more secure?

I work for myself. Every once in a while, I get an attack of fear that tells me the only way for me to be secure is to get a job. I remind myself that has been in the past, but now I make my living serving spirit. When I forget, the best way to pull me back out of that hole is doing something that lets me take the focus off my fear, such as making new cards for my Spirit Deck. I get a stack of magazines, some glue, scissors, and 5"x 7" pieces of mat board that my daughter Jenna Hill cuts for me. I tear or cut out pictures that draw my attention from the magazine and make a collage on the card. It's always amazing to me how gorgeous each final card is. And by the time I've made one or two, my fear is gone. You could use card-board or poster board instead of mat board. Have fun with your project!

Money Stories

In the movie *What the Bleep Do We Know!?* **Amit Goswami** had a small part but I thought he stood out. Soon after seeing the movie I was at a book show and saw a poster for one of his books in a publisher's booth. It turned out Amit lived just down the road in Eugene, OR, and since he was so close he was soon visiting Portland to talk about quantum physic, his ideas of how the world really works, and to introduce new books.

Amit's talks are intriguing and interesting and often filled with ideas that are hard for me to wrap my mind around at first. But after "chewing" on the ideas a bit, I get excited. I find Amit so accessible. He is someone I just want to sit and listen to over a cup of tea.

Chapter 5

Quantum Prosperity

"To me the consciousness movement means we are always exactly where we need to be. If we recognized the truth of that statement then the constant hassle of 'Should I make more money' disappears and the important question becomes 'Am I happy with what I'm doing?'" Amit Goswami

Amit Goswami, PhD, is professor emeritus in the Physics Department of the University of Oregon, where he began teaching in 1968. He is a pioneer of the new paradigm of science within consciousness. Amit has written eight popular books including *The Self-Aware Universe*, *The Visionary Window*, *Physics of the Soul*, and *Quantum Creativity*. His book *Quantum Doctor* integrates conventional and alternative medicine. Dr. Goswami calls himself a quantum activist and he appeared in the movie *What the Bleep Do We Know?!* www.dramitgoswami.com

Do you believe that money and spirituality go together?
I think the connection is more between money and happiness than money and spirituality. An old adage says "money doesn't buy happiness," but I think most people really believe that money IS synonymous with happiness and that it can buy anything. People

Money Stories

seem to feel the more material goods they have the more fulfilled they will be, but that's not accurate.

Then, there is the opposite world view, and over my lifetime I have tended toward that direction: that money means very little and is not important. That is not an accurate point of view either.

In the past, I have ignored the importance of money many times, and later regretted it. It is painfully clear that money IS needed. Without money you can still be happy, but having money can bring material comfort and add to our good health.

Neither idea, that money is everything or that money is nothing, is inaccurate. We need moderation in our money thinking. Besides the physical body, we also have a spiritual body, and ultimately, it is this spiritual side that brings us happiness.

Do you suggest we focus on the physical or spiritual parts or both?

Both the physical and spiritual bodies are part of the whole, not separate pieces, and they need to be worked with simultaneously. It is easy, though, to think of these two as separate. One of my mantras around this is "separateness is an illusion." For example, if discord and feelings of separateness arise, and believe me they do, I know it's an illusion.

Discord in my life always tells me that I need to look at or to learn something from a situation, or that a problem is trying to attract my attention. Becoming aware of what is producing the separateness or the problem gives me the opportunity to correct it.

Do you find that money and spirit or happiness work differently when another person is brought into the mix? Love relationships, relationships with kids, work relationships, so on? My experience is that dealing with money with other people can be difficult.

Issues do tend to get more complex when we get other people involved in our lives. Love relationships are not simple, even without money being added to the mix. Two people can share an experience, but we each bring our own perspective with us. Because of our different perspectives, relationships can be confusing.

How about parent-child relationships?

The parent and child are at different ages, and this bring with it different money priorities. Children usually want everything their friends have, but their parents may feel that waiting and saving is an important lesson to teach their child. The differences in both age and in priorities make parent-child relationships tricky.

As parents, we have to make our values clear and we don't make them clear just by talking. The best way to show our kids what we value is by modeling through the way we live. Then, our children can begin to see that it is not really stuff that brings happiness.

Did you have similar struggles with your children?

My relationship with my children was very checkered. I did not contribute much to their well being when they were growing up. How I lived my life when I was younger, not that I could have lived differently, is a deep regret for me. I was not who I am today.

If I could do it over again I would encourage my children to find their own way with money, from the middle ground. I'd suggest they find a place to operate that doesn't exclude the spiritual part. That part can come only when your subtle body (energy fields), mind (thinking), and vital energy (feelings and emotions) are taken care of.

Money Stories

Money brings up so many feelings. When I think of being without money it automatically brings up fear and makes my gut tighten.

That's third chakra insecurity. In other words "I need money to support myself. How do I do this, will I have enough...?" Almost every adult has some financial insecurities. We need a job. We know that having a job or a way to bring in money is essential for our well-being. Maslow's *Theory of Hierarchy* tells us that. Only when we have our physical needs met, a good job and a fair amount of money coming in, can we pay attention to our wants.

Do you feel that you are more in touch with the two sides of money and being balanced with them now than when you were younger?

Compared to how I was earlier in my life, I certainly have a different understanding now. My dilemma with money started early. For three-quarters of my academic life, I suffered a lot because of my quantum physics and consciousness research. Because of that "weird" research, my salary at the University of Oregon remained below that of an assistant professor for many years. But being tenured gave me the freedom to pursue these studies.

To me the consciousness movement means we are always exactly where we need to be. If we recognized the truth of that statement, then the constant hassle of "Should I make more money" disappears, and the more important question becomes "Am I happy with what I'm doing?"

If I'm happy, then obviously I'm where I need to be and I should continue doing it. When I'm unhappy, the relevant question is "What would make me happy?" And "How does one make more money?" is the wrong question to be asking.

Quantum Prosperity

Do money and spirituality or happiness fit into your research?

Something that has become a favorite research topic of mine is a new economics. Our capitalistic economics focuses on the material aspect of our reality, which is only a part of what economics should look at. Economics exists not just because of money, but also in terms of our well-being. Ultimately, spiritual economics would look at our physical body, and also our mind, feelings, emotions, and spiritual nature. When you consider all of these bodies, then an entirely new field called spiritual economics moves forward and I'm busy developing it. Not all of the elements are quite right yet but it is an important enterprise. There is a concerted effort on right now to find an integrated model that is more than our present capitalist model.

Capitalism, by the way, is not inconsistent with spiritual economics. It already incorporates some consciousness into it, but it's just too focused on constant growth and materialism. The question is how to improve capitalism and include these other bodies, as well as real consumer problems.

Looking at consumers as machines and trying to predict consumer spirit in that way are some of the basic failings of modern economics. We've got to add the psychology of the individual into our economic research. Can the field of spiritual economics be developed? We'll see. I think it will probably come in as the world changes. And that's just a short time away.

Things to think about:
Are you happy with your life as it is? What would you change to make your life happier? What makes you feel that life is most worthwhile? Would more money be high

Money Stories

on your list? Does your happiness have to do with how much money you have, or what possessions or people are in your life? Today, what made you feel happy or fulfilled or at peace?

Even though money is important in my life, it is not at the top of my value list. I know I need money to pay my rent and utilities, and gas for my car, and so on, but giving someone a great astrology reading, or teaching someone to make a drum or rattle that they'll love, or listening to a great audio book, or sitting down with a friend over a cup of tea is far more interesting and important.

What's on your list that makes you feel happy and fulfilled each day and how close to the top is money?

Stories of Trust

Money Stories

Tama Kieves' story about leaving her law job to be a coach and writer instantly grabbed my attention when her book and press kit ended up on my desk in 2003. I couldn't believe that someone had the courage to take such a leap of faith as to quit her job as an attorney to do what her spirit felt was a better match.

I loved hearing her story of "feeling the fear and doing it anyway" as we conversed before and after her book talk. Though it took a while for me to retire and move to this new phase of my life, (and I didn't leave hating my job), Tama's book and her story were always in the back of my mind for encouragement!

Chapter 6

Following in the Steps of Marianne Williamson

"It doesn't matter how much you are making. If you're in an incompatible job it's a spiritual wound to the soul that is not being appropriately addressed." Tama Kieves

Tama Kieves ditched her corporate law job to write and help others live their most meaningful lives. She is the author of *This Time I Dance! Creating the Work You Love (How One Harvard Lawyer Left It All to Have It All)* and her newest, *Inspired and Unstoppable: Wildly Succeeding in Your Life's Work*. She is also featured on *Oprah Radio* and is a sought-after speaker and national presenter for *A Course in Miracles*. Tama is a career and success coach, who has helped thousands worldwide discover, launch, and live their true work in the world. She is also the Founder and President of Awakening Artistry, an organization dedicated to creating and supporting a global family of visionary minds, creative souls, free-spirited entrepreneurs, and empowered leaders. www.awakeningartistry.com

Tell me what comes to mind when you think of money?
Money is energy, power, and one's expression. I've thought a lot about money, and about money and

Money Stories

spirituality, because I teach *A Course In Miracles*. When I began this career, whether to charge money for my work was important. It's spiritual work, so should you charge money for that work? Money allows me creative expression and it's an exchange of energy and power that provides the ability to interact in the world.

My decision was around valuing my work. If it is spiritual and should be free, then I'd have to get another job and wouldn't be as available to help people. I wouldn't be very spiritual or nice, and my life would be much more difficult.

How were you brought up to think of money?

I was raised orthodox Jewish, very conservatively. My parents were into saving money and being economical. We were middle class, but we didn't live that way. Sometimes, it felt like we were third-world citizens. At the end of my father's life, my mother said he wouldn't even turn on the lights; instead, he would walk around the house with a flashlight.

I tend to be good with money. In my career life, there haven't been any real money struggles, per se. My money issue was learning to spend and to let it flow away from and back to me, rather than not having enough. I needed to learn to have abundance, not via saving all of the time, but to have bounty through saving appropriately and allowing money to circulate. Learning to put my energy in what I believe in and want to support was an important lesson for me.

Typically we think of being a lawyer as more lucrative than what you are doing now.

You're right. But, in the long term of where my career will go, that won't be true. I did go to Harvard Law School and would have been a partner by now. I don't even want to think about what my income would be. But, it's been very clear that while wanting money in my life is important, it's never been a driving force or a big motivator for me.

At the end of my legal career, and now, I'd rather have starved and been poor and had the freedom to write and teach than to receive lots of money in a career that did not work for me. I love money, but it just hasn't ever been the most important thing in my life.

Has your life and your view of energy and money changed since you left your law career? Or should I say, how has it changed?

It has changed. In my legal career I wouldn't have known the word energy or even what it meant. I was very locked into what was "normal" as my source of money and value. To get money one needed a job and that meant doing something in the "known" world.

After leaving law, I'd periodically go through times of tightening and thinking "My God, what did I do?" These were periods of feeling frightened and vulnerable. I've pretty much come out the other side of those feelings, and I am more secure financially and in every other way since leaving my law job, making lots more money. My security now comes from a spiritual place, my belief in God, and my trust in the universe. When my God was money, fear was my constant companion.

Some of those changes are in my book, *This Time I Dance*. Being self-employed one can't guarantee that people will sign up for classes or coaching. Maybe people won't come back, or maybe every single one of my clients would leave. For years, when a class ended, the fear that nobody would ever sign up again would surface. But the reality was and is this amazing flow of abundance. It has always been there, and is steadily increasing.

Money Stories

So, how did you make the change? What were the things that happened to help you quit law and begin writing, teaching and coaching?

Writing has always been my dream and I didn't know how that would happen. Working as an attorney, I began shutting down, becoming depressed, and hating my life.

The biggest change was that I've always been able to "will-power" myself through anything, and that fierce determination left me. I was on billable hours and couldn't focus on reading briefs. Thank God I was smart enough to tell myself to leave voluntarily instead of being let go. "You can leave looking like a Golden Girl or you can be asked to leave. Which did you want?" I asked myself.

Leaving was not part of my plan, and it was terrifying. Who goes to Harvard Law School, graduates with honors, gets into one of the biggest law firms in the country, gets on the partnership track, and then quits? Staying one more year would have looked better on my resume. But deep in my soul, I knew I couldn't wait.

My journey has been about leaving traditional security, leaving the money, the identity, that culture, and being forced to look for inner resources, inner security, searching for my real beliefs about God, the universe, and life. One question kept coming up: "Could I do work I loved and make a living? If I was this successful doing work I didn't love, what could I do with work I did love?"

When I was growing up, my parents always made it clear that working at something fun or creative or that you love meant you were going to starve. If you want to be an artist, fine, but you'll end up a bag lady. Even so, my quest was to find my truth and inspiration.

In the Steps of Marianne Williamson

What did your family say?

You mean after screaming hysterically or the therapy bills? For a long time they thought it was just a phase. That I'd grow out of it. My family felt that being in Colorado was wild and bad enough. They were in denial at first, thinking I would get a "real job" after awhile.

My father, who was the more critical and disheartened of my parents, did say, "Well, at least you have a degree behind you so I'm not going to worry." Until he died, even though I had been out of law for years and was teaching, he'd introduce me as "my little girl, the Harvard lawyer."

Marianne Williamson was my idol. My mom didn't know who that was. "Mom, she's been on the Oprah Show," thinking that would count for something.

My family doesn't understand my work. If I say it's motivational or personal growth, my family wonders why anyone would want to do that.

How long after you left law did you begin to write and teach?

It took at least a dozen years to write my book. Believing I could write, that I had something to say and giving myself permission took that long. "There are nine million self-help books out there. Why would mine be different?" Since I didn't know anyone in that industry, how would I get published? Blah, blah, blah.

Another reason it took 12 years to write my book was that I was also developing my coaching business. My potential was clear as well as my book's possibilities, but at first I wasn't ready to step into that role. Accountability and belief in my work would be important once the book came out.

Money Stories

When I began work on my book, I lived in a studio apartment I struggled to pay for. So, it was important to absolutely be able to say with good faith, "I make every dime of my living from work I love, and that has allowed me to purchase a house and have retirement and health insurance." It took time to grow into this "bigger" person and to let go of old concerns.

Not that I completely believed in those ideas all the time, but it was important to know for myself and that I had reached my level of comfort and security. Then I could stand in front of the world and say, "Yes, this works."

It takes as long as it takes, and sometimes you have to "act as if" for a while before you get to where you want or need to be. Also, sometimes I've had to be really specific about what I need and want.

My messages to God have been on the order of "Maybe we have a different idea about what abundance means. Let's get clear. I'm willing to go out there and do this work and tell people how I made it, but not if you make me struggle. That's not very attractive in a teacher."

One of my favorite spiritual concepts is "live in a way that makes me want to know your God." It means living a life that is well rounded, loving, and flourishing on every level. That's the role model I want to be for others.

I do think we are role models and we are here to change the cultural models.

Some of the New Age and New Thought stuff was being dismissed as too woo-woo or pie-in-the-sky. I wanted to give legitimacy to spirituality and creativity, to show these ideas are not frivolous or from people who can't cope. These spiritual and creative tools are incred-

In the Steps of Marianne Williamson

ible resources that we haven't fully utilized. They can expand our reality and our expressiveness. But, for me, guys in orange robes don't work as role models. Marianne Williamson did and was the role model I craved. She looked normal, was making it, and she believed in this stuff. And she wore makeup. I could embrace that.

Now, my definitions have expanded. It's important to live in the world in a way that can reach people. In many spiritual, artistic, and writing communities, people squeak by. These limitations are not necessarily what Spirit would ask of us. My personal goal is abundance.

I tell people there are no starving artists, but, though not monetarily, there are starving attorneys. I was impoverished as an attorney, even though a lot more financial resources were available to me. You get trapped by the money. Lots of my present clients are in that place. Some make more money than I'll ever see and many of those have less abundance than me. Theoretically, they make more but they're in debt or over spend or have health problems. Misery costs you.

It doesn't matter how much you are making. If you're in an incompatible job it's a spiritual wound to the soul that is not being appropriately addressed. If you buy more shoes, will the wound be addressed? And how many pairs of shoes can you wear at one time?

Things to think about:
Are you in a job that is incompatible with your values and/or your spirituality? Are there ways to make that job more compatible? What changes do you need to make? What will it take to make these changes?

If it's not possible to make your present job compatible, what would your ideal job look like? Make a

Money Stories

list of the 50 important aspects of your perfect job. Close your eyes and picture yourself in that job, then write about how you feel each day when you get up and go to your new job and how you feel at the end of the day. What are your daily tasks, what does your work space look and feel like, how does your first paycheck look and feel, and so on? The clearer your mental picture the more accessible your vision will be.

Back in 1994 I kept "seeing" myself in a book store job. I made a list of what I wanted in that job and wrote about how it felt to be there. I "knew" that I was headed in that direction and could feel myself in a book store position. I applied for several openings at one book store and wasn't even called for an interview and was beginning to feel disillusioned. But when I finally heard there was an opening at New Renaissance Bookshop, I knew that was my job. I kept "imagining" myself there through the interview process. I heard, later, that several dozen people had applied, but I just kept seeing myself employed there and that visioning or imagining worked!

Money Stories

I met **James Wanless** at an International New Age Trade Show in Denver. I had just been introduced to his *Voyager Tarot Deck* and was trying to understand how these cards, which were collage images, related to the traditional *Rider-Waite Deck* I had learned on. James was doing mini-readings at his publisher's booth and when I walked by, since no one was waiting, I slipped in for a reading. I don't remember the cards that were pulled, but I know they were probably the Goddess or the Moon card because these became my identity, seeming to come up in almost all of his future readings for me. I was amazed with James's readings. He always asked questions that pointed me in exciting new and bigger directions than I would ever have allowed myself to imagine.

Just before I left New Renaissance, James gave me a reading that let me know I was moving in the right direction and that all would work out for my best and highest good.

Chapter 7

Money in My Cards

> *"When you said money, the first thing that came to mind, and it always comes to my mind, is that word* manna. *Kind of a Hawaiian word, grace and abundance from great spirit, the gods and goddesses. Manna is a sense of richness and life energy."* James Wanless, Ph.D

James Wanless was a distinguished university professor in the Middle East when he experienced a life-threatening disease that led to a spiritual transformation. James let go of his academic career and began sharing his newfound wisdom through *The Voyager Tarot Deck*. He is also the author of *Way of the Great Oracle: Strategic Intuition for the 21st Century, New Age Tarot, Wheel of Tarot,* and *Intuition@Work*. James is often called "Mr Tarot" because of his enormous contribution to that field. He is a master Tarot reader, has created online courses in Tarot, and has developed a technique of using the Tarot as a proactive tool for Fortune Creation and Life Coaching. www.jameswanless.com

As we begin talking, pull a card about what money and spirituality mean for you. From knowing you for a number of years, I get a strong feeling that money and spirituality work well in your life, that you may have had some strug-

Money Stories

gles with them, but that they work well most of the time. Wow, you pulled the Sun card! Tell me what that means.

The sun is energy, so it's all combined. Money is a form of energy The sun is energy. Why are there so many hang-ups about money? I know mine are there because I grew up with money hang-ups. I can't really recall any negative money experience, just some attitudes. The Sun card makes me feel "Wow! There is money in that card and it's all gold!"

I look at the card and see how vibrant the colors are. When you talk about money as energy, the colors express that.

You can't get clearer than this card. To be the Sun, and one could be the sun as a parent to a child or a guru to a disciple or teacher to a student or boss to employee. In my work I see myself as the sun. I send out lots of light and energy. I need food in return, in the form of people liking my work or receiving value from it, and me being rewarded, financially. Then I'm able to put out more light. The more you put in the more you get out. So, money is a good thing, but I must say it's not my highest priority.

Have you had times in your life when you struggled to have enough money?

It's always been a bit of a struggle. I was an academic and they don't make much money. Then, I go into this so-called *spiritual field*, which is a poverty field for lots of people, as well, though I don't see it that way. The attitudes are "You'd better be poor, and if not, you have contaminated the purity of the spiritual path." That's Old World thinking!

What we are doing, and I count myself in that field too, is that our job is to change that Old World paradigm.

I'm not a materialist. Stuff is heavy and hard to carry around and my life is not about having money for stuff. It's about having money for experiences, like trav-

Money in My Cards

el or getting my dream house. When you said money, the first thing that came to mind and it always comes to my mind is that word *manna*. Kind of a Hawaiian word for grace and abundance from great spirit, the gods and goddesses. Manna is a sense of richness and life energy. Such power comes from that manna, having that power and right now.

I live such a rich life. Looking at the actual money I make, it's not six figures, yet my home is in Carmel, I travel the world, I wear pretty cool clothes, my friends are great, I go to the beach. I can't imagine a richer life. So, is it always the actual amount of money?

That's an interesting point. I see how much I make and how much a lot of people around me make and my income is substantially less than theirs. But I am pretty satisfied.

Just because you make more money doesn't mean anything about happiness. I would never want to live the lives of some of my richest friends. It's not about the money per se; it's more about your attitude about the money, what you do with it, and what value it has. Some so-called rich people have many employees working on their houses and gardens and so on, and they have no privacy. There's all this responsibility. Who needs that? Maybe freedom *is* when you have nothing else to lose. Maybe ultimate freedom is being a monk or something like that.

That is true. As a monk you don't have to worry about money. Someone else takes care of the money. So what is your view of spirituality? You talked about money as energy. Do the two fit together for you?

Spirit is the life force. What makes the life force? The sun! What makes the life force go around in our world? There is inspiration, there is motivation, there's creativity, and work, and all that, and the thing that greases the wheel is money. Intrinsically, both are en-

Money Stories

ergy. From a spiritual viewpoint, I feel that everything is connected.

Why is money any different from any other spiritual value? Like enlightenment? To me enlightenment and richness are the same thing. Different facets of the same life force, so no real difference. No disconnect. At the same time, knowing that, money, in itself, still doesn't drive me. Doing something creative and acting on inspiration drives me much more than money. Money is certainly an incredible spiritual value for me, but not my number-one value.

So, you'd say that creativity is a lot higher on your value scale than money?

If you are creative, you are alive. If you are rich, you're not necessarily alive. You may just be sitting there with a Swiss bank account, counting your money and doing nothing else. Having money has no value. It's what you do with it that has value. To me, it all goes back to being creative and following inspiration. My best friends are teachers, people who are acting with inspiration regardless of how much money they have or don't have. That's what I look at in people, that quality of richness.

When I was growing up, our minister used to give sermons about tithing and service three or four times a year. He'd tell us that it was our duty to tithe or to give 10% of our income to the church. I think it was probably hard for him to talk about money, but he felt it was necessary to bring in the funds for his salary and the upkeep of the church.

When did the divorce between church, spirit, and money begin? I think it's a Christian thing. Then again, look at the Buddha. He walked away from his palace and all of his riches to be poor and to beg for food.

Money in My Cards

Another value issue is how much to charge for your services. A reading could change a person's life and it could be invaluable. How much do you charge for that? My rates could be higher and that would have value, because the more people pay, the more they value a service. At the same time, I want to be accessible. Not everyone can afford to come to me now, but my rates are accessible to most people and being accessible to most people is one of my values.

I could charge more, but it all comes back to value. By charging $500 an hour, I'd cut out a lot of people. I'd rather be of service and reach more people.

It might be that you charge one group of people one thing and another group another price.

I always offer scholarships. That's one way I can reach a larger population.

I've found that some practitioners are very wound up in how much they charge and others don't care. Some may say, "Oh, it has to be this much." But they are upset if people don't sign up for sessions. Since we are talking about what you charge, do you vary your rates in various parts of the country?

Absolutely, my fees are varied. If I work in Santa Cruz, with a lot of students, my rates are less than, say, in New York or Los Angeles. But most of my readings come from my website and my web rates are standard.

But with money, I never even balance my check book because I don't want to spend the time doing that. Other activities have more value for me.

What a lot of us are about, moving into our second half of life, second career, boomers who want to re-fire and not retire, is right livelihood, which is finding work that is purposeful, passionate, playful, growthful as a spiritual path, and prosperous or profitable: the p-words.

Money Stories

It's a balance. I think you could work spiritually and make a ton of money. And some people work just to live. I've seen people manipulate others on the spiritual path to make a lot of money.

What we are talking about here is the balance of it all. The wholeness of it. The flowering of it. Like petals on a flower and each petal has a purpose. I like the play and the pathness and profitability of it. That to me is richness.

I like people making money; however, a lot of people don't make money that has meaning other than to get stuff and have a bigger this or that. It's about the quality, not the quantity. The quality is a lot more intrinsic. It's not about a bank account. But people in America judge by how much and how big.

I was voted the most likely to succeed in my high school class. I know for a fact that my income is less than most who come to reunions, yet my life and my lifestyle are so enjoyable to me. In a sense, I have succeeded in very rich ways. The richest guy in our class started a bank and no one likes him. Does it mean there's a disconnect between likability and money? I think it's the whole social thing about money.

Could you let it all go? Some rich people could. Saying that, I don't know if I could let everything go. I like having a car and a house. I do think though about what it would be like to be Peace Pilgrim? What would it be like to walk until someone offered you a bed? What an incredibly rich way to live!

That's the real spiritual test. Do you trust? Do you believe? Maybe that's the rite of passage that we should move toward.

I like the idea that we have to make money. That is the "mother or father" of invention. I like, that in my

Money in My Cards

60s, I still have to make money and can't afford to retire. But I don't mind because I love my work, and I like being driven to do it, and that I still like it. Needing money really does force us to do something.

I love the drive to make money. In nature it's a built-in drive to "make a living." The birds and animals get their food and whatever they need for life instead of money. They don't look for extra, just enough for now. Our problem is that we are always looking for more than we need. Another TV in each room. We try to keep up with our neighbors or friends; "How come we aren't making as much or more than they are?" Then money becomes the issue rather than what we are doing for it.

Do you have worries about retirement?

Hell yes! But I trust. I may be able to work until I'm 90. But I have to be smart enough. I have to think about how I can continue to work for 20 more years.

The money thing is really interesting because it is probably the one area that is the most out of balance for us. It's where I have the greatest deprivation or lack. I can complain about it, but at the same time I don't care. There is so much cultural and family stuff about making money, but my family was not moneyed. My grandfather was knighted because he was a medical missionary in India. My father never talked about money. Nobody really talked or thought about it. But I live in a moneyed society. What needs to change? I'm making more money and am amping up my work at all levels. I want more clients, and to do better work, and to grow, and why not?

Maybe, if there was no issue about money, I could say "I'm raising my prices way up and that's the way it is. It's all about money now." I wonder how that would feel. Part of me goes into fear that nobody would

Money Stories

show up. My fear is that my readings and my work are not worth that much. Frankly, I think my work is way more valuable than what I get paid for it. You probably think the same thing.

Yes, and I wish that people like us, and teachers, and daycare workers, all of us would get paid what we were worth. To a large extent I don't worry about money either, but I do when an unexpected bill comes in. For the most part I do trust and the money comes in when it's needed.

No kidding. I've been on my own for 30 years in the world of Tarot, which is a pretty funky way to make a living. It's the craziest kind of work to do. But I live from month to month, and trust. When you are always on the edge financially, you do have to trust. It makes you more aware of how this world works, energetically. Amazing!

I do know that my richest friends are people who want to make money, and that was their goal. So success follows interest. Duh!

What is our number-one value? It may not be about making money. For me that number one is authenticity. If money is your thing then do it. No judgment. I love all my friends, *authentically!*

Things to think about:
What do you value most in your life? Is money the most important thing or is it something like family or feeling fulfilled or happiness or creativity or being in touch with spirit or freedom? Get out your favorite oracle such as Tarot cards, runes, or the *I Ching*. Ask the question "What do I value?" Then draw a card, pick a rune, throw the coins, or do whatever your oracle asks you to do and see what comes up. How does this card relate to what you value? Contemplate this question as you

go about your day and see what answers or questions come to you.

I use many oracles, including a deck that I made. Each helps me in a different way. I use the *Russian Gypsy Fortune Telling Deck* at the beginning of each new year to give me hints about the upcoming year. I use the *I Ching* when I've been stuck for a while. And I use my deck for every day or when I'm about ready to do a reading or teach someone to make a drum or rattle. They always give me new insights and help me release stuck energy.

Money Stories

Since my first cultural anthropology classes, I've always felt a kinship with the ideas of coyote energy, something backwards or unpredictable or that could not be controlled. When I first heard of **Lewis Mehl-Madrona,** it was seeing the title of his book *Coyote Medicine* in the Bear & Co. catalogue. My first thought was "I want to meet this man."

Then, at a book show I saw a poster for the book in the booth. Since Lewis lived on the other side of the country, I couldn't imagine him being able to visit Portland, but it ended up that he had a buddy who lived in Portland and it was a convenient stop on his way to visit his son, so I got to meet this "master" of coyote energy up close at a book talk. After that first talk, Lewis became a regular visitor on his trips to the West Coast. Lewis tells stories like a medicine man that show how real healing works. His goal is to marry present-day and native healing teachings in a very non-traditional way.

Chapter 8

Releasing Struggles

"We somehow need to work toward a different relationship to money. A big part is to learn to cooperate."
Lewis Mehl-Madrona

Lewis Mehl-Madrona's goals include a paradigm shift within medicine, psychiatry, and psychology toward aligning with indigenous knowledge systems, and the use of complexity theory and quantum physics concepts to explore our world and to help each other to heal, grow, and change. Lewis teaches Biological Basis of Behavior, Statistics, Narrative Theory and Therapy, Professionalization Seminars, and Research Methodology at the Union Institute and the University in Brattleboro, Vermont. His books include *Coyote Medicine, Coyote Healing, Coyote Wisdom,* and *Narrative Medicine.* www.mehl-madrona.com

Tell me how money works in your life.
Having not enough money and struggling to get more has always been my relationship with money. Then, a few years back I just came to the conclusion that probably if I stopped struggling, there still might not be enough, and I'd still want more, but I'd be happier.

Money Stories

From then on I stopped struggling. Things haven't really changed; well, more money is coming in now than back then. I'm on a salary. So what has really changed is that I'm more peaceful about money now. There are the usual collection of demands and people who want thing from me. But in terms of my life, it's fairly simply and focused on things that are important to me. We choose what we think is significant.

Do you see a connection between money and spirituality in your life?

Only in the sense that whenever I've done something just for the money, it has always been a really bad idea. Those are the things that backfire. Sometimes doing things and not caring about the money is a really fun way to go. And other times I'm surprised and someone actually pays me, and sometimes they don't.

I think the spiritual part is letting go of the attachment. Thich Nhat Hanh tells a story about Buddha and a farmer.

Buddha and his disciples are sitting by the road talking and being happy and doing what teachers and disciples do. Then a farmer runs up to them and frantically asks "Have you seen my cows? Have you seen my cows? I've lost them."

Buddha says "No. I'm sorry, we haven't seen them."

Finally, the farmer finds the cows and everything is fine. But Buddha and his disciples are there for a week and this happens four or five times during the week. Finally, Buddha says to his disciples, "It doesn't seem like having cows is a very good thing."

I spent a year camping out, sometimes sleeping in my car. It was a really helpful year for me, though it wasn't all that much fun, but I learned how to do it. I

Releasing Struggles

could get by with very little. It makes me think about people I know who live simply in Mexico or Cuba. You know, we suffer so much from the fear that we won't have enough, that by the time we don't have enough, it's a let-down.

Letting go has always been difficult for me. Letting go or non-attachment is big, and also hard to do, but once I allow it, miracles almost always happen.

It's funny how that works. I remember doing a workshop for a friend. I wasn't expecting to get paid. At the end he gave me an envelope containing $5000. I said, "Are you nuts?"

He said "No, no. I'm rich and just wanted you to have it."

I remember being in private practice. Reminding people to pay, and putting a price on my work. It's really difficult. My intensives still have to be priced, but I do it by asking myself "How much do I need to charge and not feel resentful doing this work?"

That's how intensives are priced now. I have a job and get paid and don't have to do anything else and that's part of it, too. I don't have to do intensives, but doing roughly one a month is still fun. They end up being about five hours a day of my time for the week. These seminars are a lot of work but also a lot of fun. I ask myself, "Since my other work still has to be done, how much do I need to charge to be happy doing this extra work? "

If somebody says the intensive costs too much, I respond, "That's what I need for this extra thing and I don't want to do it for less because I'll feel resentful."

Being aware if something makes me feel resentful or not certainly makes me feel more peaceful. It's a

Money Stories

good thing. Anger, bitterness, and resentment are all toxic waste products that I don't want in my life.

I've heard you tell a story about teaching an intensive and saying to the group, "This is how much I need to teach this intensive. You guys divide it up how you want." We tend to be too afraid to do that kind of thing, because it won't be fair.

That workshop was so stress-free and they figured it out. I didn't have to do anything with the individual pricing.

Can you talk more about what 'enough' means to you?' It's one of the things lots of people work on, how to feel like they have enough. Enough house, enough time, or enough money. How did you come to that point that you just let it go?

It happened during my year of car-camping. I was doing that so that my almost ex-wife could live well while taking care of our son. My needs were small. My son needed a nice place to live and his mom had other children. So, no big deal.

At the time my work was for this profit-making corporation that was supposed to be my bridge to an academic job, but it turned out not to be. It felt like I was working for evil capitalists. They didn't want to pay me for charting patient information and quibbled over nearly everything.

Once I drove to a clinic that was two hours away and they had closed for the day because of the cold. They didn't tell me and then didn't want to pay me for the day's work. I said "You hired me for the day of work and didn't tell me you were closing or give me a chance to line up some other work."

Their position was "Too bad for you."

If a patient didn't show, they didn't want to pay me. There was a point where suing these people felt like

Releasing Struggles

the only way, and I looked into it. But it changed my energy so much just thinking about suing them. So my question for myself was "What if you just let it all go? What if you just stopped caring about all of this?"

Here I was living in a car. It was my almost ex-wife who was getting most of the financial benefit of my labor. The only thing I was doing was occasionally eating and working a lot.

So, I found a salaried academic job that in the end actually paid a little more than the for-profit place, because I wasn't being nickeled and dimed all the time. And actually my salary at the new job was a little more, but my perspective was that it didn't matter.

Now, I mentor medical students. One of the things I tell them is that freedom is more important than the money. Medical students are offered all of these loans to get fancy cars and stuff that they won't have to start paying for until graduation. But when they graduate, you won't believe the debt burden they'll have.

I tell students this is what they do to doctors. They put them on the debt tread-mill. Once you are on that path, you don't get off until you have your heart attack or you burn out or collapse.

I tell students to resist temptation. Freedom is more important than money. That is what I got from my car-camping year. At that point, there were hungry mouths to feed and I was aware of that. But we'd all survive if I couldn't do it anymore. I wasn't willing to work in that evil environment. Luckily, a nice academic job came to me. Now I'm happy and make a good living.

If something else came up that I wanted to do that was lower pay, I'd do it, and somehow, we'd all get by.

Money Stories

We somehow need to work toward a different relationship to money. A big part is to learn to cooperate. There's that "Prisoner's Game," also called "The Money Game." You get paid to make different decisions. And you always get the longest-term benefit by cooperating instead of trying to out-maneuver people or strategize by aligning yourself with one person one time and another person another time.

The game is from Economics 101. It teaches people that there is more to cooperation than meets the eye. Students forget the game when they reach MBA 101.

Somehow, we have to create more opportunities to cooperate so we can see that it's fun. Win-win is fun. We are taught that win-lose is the most fun. If somebody wins, then someone else has to lose. I don't know when we'll get more into cooperation but from my vantage point it's crucial.

Cooperation is such a great concept, and it feels so far away from where we are today.

It has certainly been useful to me to stay out of situations that bring me resentment and to realize how good it feels doing things I love that may not be terribly profitable, because in those cases the money is secondary.

At this point I have enough friends for me to do "an Arthur Miller." When Arthur was a starving author in Paris, he had 40 friends he would stay with every 40th night. He said that was about the right ratio because people looked forward to your entertaining stories and after 40 nights you had new material to deliver in payment for their couch. I could probably do that now. Or I could live on the beach in Mexico.

At first, hearing your car-camping story, my thought was that I couldn't live in my car. But then again it sounds really freeing to own only what could fit in your car.

Releasing Struggles

Possessions are like balls and chains. The more you have, the more space you need, and it gets old.

Things to think about:
What in your life makes you feel resentful or irritated or depressed or sad or angry, guilty, or numb? How would your life change if you no longer felt this way. What brings out these feelings for you? Without burying them what can you do to prevent them?

It's normal to occasionally feel resentment, anger, sadness, or even depression, but when these feelings continue to occur or occur every time you do certain things, that's the time to look at those situations and see how they can be released or changed. Can you change your point of view so that you have the power to say "no" to something that is keeping you from experiencing more joy and/or experiencing life more fully? What would that look like?

Money Stories

I met **Maridel Bowes** when Hal Zina Bennet referred her to me to do a talk about her "grandma book" (*Who Are You Calling Grandma?*). When I found that she was also an astrologer, we had lots to talk about and became great friends. A reading from Maridel helped me know it was time to retire from New Renaissance Bookshop and begin my next step with astrology, drumming, drum and rattle making, and working on this book.

Maridel lived in California when we first met and came up to Oregon from time to time to visit her sons. We always managed a cup of coffee or tea or lunch and a chat. Then, she moved down the road to Dundee, Oregon. In the course of our chats, Maridel told me some of her fascinating abundance stories and I knew they had to be part of this book!

Chapter 9

Provision

"I've had provision all my life but I believe the new level of it really goes back to deciding not to worry about money. That was a big turning point." Maridel Bowes

Maridel Bowes' life journey took her from the Bible Belt, and a papa who was a preacher, to California for marriage, kids, a counseling practice, astrology, and teaching, and then to Oregon to write and be part of her grand-babies' lives. Over the years she has done Evolutionary Astrology readings and taught classes, including Breathing Free, which uses Holotropic Breathwork. Now she is tapping into the notion of "Provision" and how we can be and are provided for. Maridel published her first book, *Who Are You Calling Grandma?* in 2006. In 2010, she published her second book, *Houses of My Consciousness*, for and with her mother. So now, as she says at the end of her web contact page at www.evolvingjourney.com, the journey continues...

Let's talk about how money works in your life. You told me that you had made a decision to stop worrying about money. How did you do that?

It was one of those routine moments. On my way to Trader Joe's one day, I realized I was worrying

Money Stories

about whether I had enough money for my purchases. At that point I had an epiphany that I had worried about money all my life, and yet provision had always been there, often well beyond my needs. At that moment it was apparent that worrying was useless and served no purpose. It wasn't contributing anything positive, and in fact, was detrimental. Trips to Trader Joe's have always been fun, but if I'm worrying, the trips aren't enjoyable.

So I decided to teach myself to stop worrying. If I'm okay in the moment, and I was, and in reflection always had been, why give up that experience to not being okay? That was the basis of my learning to stop worrying. I kept coming back to the notion of being okay right now, and asking why it would be any other way in five minutes or five days?

When larger challenges came up, I found the same principles worked. As you know, when embarking on something new, challenges come up to test the new thoughts. Sometimes I'd need to touch into the feeling of being okay several times in an hour. But what I found, was that even if the challenge was formidable, worrying still didn't help.

It was foolish to worry about money even when there was a sense that I might not be okay, like the scary time my partner Johnny lost his job, and it was up to me to create all our funds. Worrying contributed nothing. If I worried, it took away my capacity to create a solution, not from my head, but from my spirit.

Most of us do worry. I don't think we imagine it's going to help, but it's almost like sleeping, eating, or breathing. It's this part of us we don't even consider doing in another way.

Recently, I saw a vivid example of worrying in a doctor's waiting room. Someone walked in and knew

Provision

the couple sitting next to me. Catching up, the new person asked the husband "How's your job in this economy?"

He said, "Well, there are some changes going on in the company, but I'm not really worried."

His wife said, "He doesn't have to. I do that for him."

The other woman said, "Well, somebody has to do it!"

There it was! This assumption that we have to worry about money. I think too about the conversations that occur in our culture about what you would do if you were to win the lottery and why you wish you would. For many, it's so they wouldn't have to worry about money anymore.

And what you hear is that many lottery winners end up worse off than they were before.

That's right. It again brings us up against the assumption that worry is necessary.

Since you work for yourself doing readings, you can't say "I need seven readings this week to pay my bills, and they come. I shouldn't say they don't come, but it's one of those things that you can't count on unless you are in a position where you have a waiting list. Have you had times since training yourself not to worry that you have come up against not having the money you needed? Since your tendency in the past would have been to worry, how do you handle those times now?

I have a base income, but it doesn't cover all of my expenses. So, I'm only partially dependent on readings for my livelihood.

Ordinarily, the readings are there and fortunately it isn't seven a week! Yet, when I've done the last reading in the queue, I would catch myself moving toward worry. At those times I get to look at my assumption

Money Stories

that readings are the only source of my income or provision. That's an example of how narrow my perspective can be with money.

Gosh, I've been provided for in lots of different ways over the years. When I would open up to that provision, either readings and/or some other source of income would come. Or a bill came later than expected or was paid another way. Sometimes it was the ability to borrow short term until my base money came in.

My friend Sandy and I have been friends for 25 years and shared a house in the past. We have this ongoing soulful relationship. Sandy has made it clear that any time I need to borrow it's alright, but it's my least favorite way to handle things. Then again, it's provision, and it's there until the money would come in and I'd be able to pay her back and move on. The universe has been exceedingly creative.

There again, it's catching those limitations. Worry is a limitation, and so is believing that money or provision can come from only one source.

I like that. Last year I quit a part-time job to focus on my own work. I decided to use some retirement funds to supplement what was coming in. The money lasted less time than anticipated because I had some unexpected expenses for classes I was teaching. My first thought was that I needed to get a new part-time job. But I decided to just wait and see what happened. Every once in a while I'd go look on Craigslist and then I'd think "I don't want to work for anyone else" and income would come in. It's funny about how money stretches and can be more magical than I ever thought. You have a great magical story about selling your trailer. Can you share that story?

I had this darling little mobile home at Dillon Beach, California, where I wrote *Who Are You Calling*

Provision

Grandma? After writing the book, I moved to Fresno and it was so far to the beach that I just didn't go much and the space rent was several hundred dollars a month.

I told a friend I was thinking about getting rid of the trailer and she asked if she could go in on it with me. She ended up buying half of the trailer and paying half of the space rent. Later, when I couldn't even continue to pay half of the rent, she took over the entire payments. When she bought a bigger trailer, we had to get rid of my little one, and selling it was complicated because the wheels were rusted and wouldn't turn anymore.

We met to talk about the selling details and she suggested putting it on Craigslist. She had a picture we could use. Since it would have to be taken out on a flatbed truck, my friend suggested we just give it away. I thought about it, but ended up listing it for $1000.

A flood of people wanted to bring me cash sight unseen. I told one person he could have the trailer, but then I didn't hear back from him.

Then, I got an email request that was totally different from the others. It said "This would be an answer to our prayers. Our home burned down and since then we've been sharing a one-bedroom apartment with our in-laws." He could come up that evening from the Bay area with the money.

I told the man the trailer had been promised to someone else and I had to give the other person some time to get back to me. I suggested we meet at the trailer that Saturday. Then I wrote to the other guy and said if I didn't hear back from him by a certain time it was going to someone else. I literally sat and watched the clock but no response.

My friend and I met the couple at the trailer and they gave us a thousand dollars in cash that their family

Money Stories

had collected. The couple was thrilled with the trailer and told me where they were going to put it and that they were going to live in it until they could build a house on some family land. I cleared out the trailer and they promised to keep in touch.

Then, I got an email from the husband saying an uncle had come and they were able to pull the trailer out and didn't need a flat bed. Somehow they got the wheels to turn!

It's so amazing that we all got what we needed. Another crucial piece was that if we hadn't sold the trailer, it would have needed to be hauled out and dumped, and that would cost at least $500. Since the inside was perfect, it would have been heart-breaking to have to dump it.

All the way around it was one of those stories where everybody benefitted. I wrote a story about the experience called *Destiny at Dillon Beach*. It was one of those miraculous stories of provision.

I'm getting ready to write again and I think provision may be my topic. Looking back over my life I've had such powerful experiences, not relate only to money but related to things that money isn't even part of. So often abundance is equated only with money, but that's just one facet of abundance.

The place you're in right now is another example of provision, don't you think?

Provision comes in many forms. Getting this place is another incredible story. I'm not in a little dumpy one-bedroom apartment. I'm in this beautiful place on this beautiful property for less than a dumpy apartment would cost me. And, in fact, my electricity and wifi are part of the rent. Our culture is all about needing millions. I'm realizing there's nothing wrong with having

Provision

a million dollars, but you don't need to have a million dollars to have what is important to you. There is something very magical about provision and I feel like my life is magical.

So now in your life you are getting ready to start a new project and you have moved into this new apartment. How did you decide to make these changes?

Just a few weeks before my move, I was really happy in a wonderful condo and felt gratitude every day. There are lots of astrological aspects hitting into my chart, and I've been immersing myself in Hawaiian spirituality and working with different frequencies, so it doesn't take much for me to hear Spirit speaking now. What came through was that it was time to make a change. I stopped my social media activities (I know it will be useful in the future and there will be a purpose for me to have learned it), stopped blogging, stopped my newsletter. Nothing was coming. It was like trying to write through water. Even though it's hard for me not to be writing, the feelings were strong to just let go and surrender. Doing all that felt right and wonderful because astrology supports me.

The next thing that came from Spirit was that I was going to be writing in 2012. Not just the blog and newsletter but a book project. I didn't even know my topic, but the feelings were strong.

I agreed that everything was negotiable except living close to my grand-kids. It was apparent that I was supposed to be there. Everything else went on the table for change, including my condo. Rent would have to be significantly less for me to move and not do readings or do very minimal readings.

I was on my way to Sacramento. While there, I talked with a few close friends who were very support-

Money Stories

ive of my new direction. Writing ideas was another topic of our conversation and provision and not worrying about money was one topic that came up. I had given a talk on that so maybe it could be turned into a book. My plan was to do little or no astrology. My friend thought maybe the writing and astrology were supposed to go together.

The next morning my friend said that during the night she'd gotten a very clear picture of me writing a series of books, not about astrology but related to astrology. I came back from Sacramento feeling energized. In a week my direction had deepened and been confirmed. The move and my writing topic were becoming clearer. Looking on Craigslist, there was nothing that cut my rent enough in the Apartment Section. But, under Spaces and Exchanges I found a listing called a "spacious studio, attached to a home on two acres of land."

I read the description and looked at the pictures. That it was furnished set me back at first. Having my own things was important to me. But the rent was a little over half of my present rent, and it included Wifi and electricity. It hit me that even doing no readings I'd have more money than now.

Was this the next step on my path? I emailed the people but didn't hear back right away. Then my computer crashed, and it was difficult to pursue. But a couple of days later an email finally came saying the place was still available, but someone was considering it. The landlord invited me to come look at the place though.

All of a sudden my message was "Oh, my God, this is it." So, I went and looked at it.

Right away the woman let me know she wouldn't need to charge me the $37.50 for a background

Provision

check because she sensed I was a trustworthy person. We stood there talking about it as if it was done.

I told her I'd need time to talk to my present landlord before giving her a move-in date. But they still hadn't heard from the other person who was interested, so she needed to give him time to decide. That took me back because I didn't want to hear they had another person who might get it. I drove away thinking "what is this?" but at the same time I had a sense the place was mine. That night I sent her an email saying I was trusting in the highest good for all concerned. The next day she wrote me back saying they had not heard from the other person and were moving forward with me.

I still needed to let the condo landlord know about my move; he is such a sweet young man who had been so attentive and responsive. He told the new people I was a great tenant and would be missed. Great reference!

That was such a big change and it sounds like it sure moved quickly!

So, here's what the timing looked like: On October 22nd, I came back from Sacramento and November 22nd I moved! I guess when you say 'okay' to Spirit and put everything on the table, things move fast! Patrick, my former landlord, told me three times he knew our paths would cross again. It really touched me.

The new people have been wonderful, too. I had one of those radiator-like heaters that didn't heat well. Most of the heat is supposed to come from the house, but they use a fireplace insert and don't use the furnace much. So the radiator was not up to the job. I mentioned it and that the hot plate knob was missing. That night the new landlord showed up with a new smart heater, a double hot plate, and because he knew that I liked

Money Stories

tea, an electric tea kettle. That is another example of provision. I didn't have to buy those things. They were brought to me!

It just shows me that this is all magic. I've had provision all my life, but I believe this new level of provision really goes back to deciding not to worry about money. That was a big turning point in my life.

Things to think about:
What does provision look like in your life? Does it come from having a job or an inheritance or a partner or parents who provide for you? What is the difference between need and want? Is provision equal to what you need or want, or both? Are all of your needs provided for? Are all of your wants satisfied? What happens if you need something and you don't have it? Do you worry if your needs are not taken care of? Does worrying help or hinder the situation?

Try spending a few minutes not worrying. How does the worried feeling differ from the non-worried feeling? Use your journal to record your answers to the questions and the difference in your worried and non-worried states. Use words or pictures in your journal to record your answers.

I have found that when I begin to worry or feel fear, it signals me to look inside and see what is going on. What is the worry really about? As Maridel says, "I've always been taken care of." Going to my gym or for a walk or doing something different will take me out of that fear place and help me look at what is really going on. Just stopping for a minute and doing something else almost always brings me answers.

Stories of Faith

Money Stories

I met **Carol Redmond** my first day at New Renaissance Bookshop back in 1995. Carol began working at the store a week before I did so we were trained on most things at the same time. During this time we learned how to use the computer system, to sort and shelve books, the book categories and tricks for finding lost or mis-shelved items, and how to work with customers. Carol and I found our niches at this time: Carol working more with the book side and I, more with the non-book or gift areas.

When Carol moved to North Carolina, we stayed in touch by email and occasionally by phone. And when she traveled back to the Portland area, we always got together. During one of these trips, she told me her story of getting the money to buy her cabins, and of course it needed to be part of this book. Thanks for sharing your story, Carol.

Chapter 10

An Angel at My Door

"Frankly, money has never been a problem. It's there when it's needed and I've never been other than blessed and graced by that gift. If I trust and turn my life over to God, seriously, what is needed comes." Carol Redmond

Carol Redmond and I both worked at New Renaissance Bookshop for a few years, and then left. When Carol left Portland she found Black Mountain, North Carolina to be a perfect place for the rest and relaxation she needed. Now the owner of Cabin Creek Lodge, Carol welcomes U.S. and international guests to her cabins. She is an avid hiker and can point you to trails that fit your style, whether an easy stroll or a steep trek. Carol has also traveled the world as a delegate for the sport of synchronized swimming after being honored as a Hall of Fame member. She was a member of the Ananda communities in California and in Portland.
www.cabincreeklodge.com

How do money and spirituality work in your life, or do they?

My biggest priority was to establish my spirituality. Then everything else fell in place. I don't want to generalize for others, but for me, when I finally allowed

Money Stories

God to run things, everything else in my life came along and began to work well.

Frankly, money has never been a problem. It's there when it's needed and I've never been other than blessed and graced by that gift. If I trust and turn my life over to God, seriously, what is needed comes. I don't have a money plan, except just day to day. It's simply not a worry.

Can you give me an example of how trust works for you?

My favorite story is how Cabin Creek Lodge came to me. I'd owned the bed & breakfast next door for seven years, then my parents decided to move here so I could help Mom take care of Dad. We planned to build a house for them behind the B-&-B, but only two extra buildings were allowed on the property. There were already two trailers, one for my handyman and the other for a pregnant single gal with a blind daughter. Both were great friends and it was difficult to decide who to give notice to.

One morning I woke up and Pine Lodge (the old name of the cabins) popped into my mind. The cabins had been for sale for some time and the owner was a friend. Until that morning I'd never given Pine Lodge a second thought but I decided to go look at the cabins. After talking, we made a handshake deal for me to buy them though I had no idea where the money was going to come from.

The sale depended on several things. First, could the owner carry back part of the money so that the bank could have some equity? Second, the bank needed to think the property was worth the price. And third, my handyman and his family needed to be interested in moving into the main house and managing the cabins for me, while I continued to manage the B-&-B.

An Angel at My Door

My handyman loved the idea. He had wanted to start his own handyman business and there would be at least a year's worth of work for him on the cabins.

A letter of intent was drawn up. The owner didn't want to close until her season ended in December and it was July. So I had six months to find the money.

The handyman would become the manager, and he and his family were excited because they'd get to move out of their trailer. My parents were excited because we could begin building their house. It was working out really well.

Getting the financing is the interesting part of my story though. My B-&-B is far enough out of town that it didn't get drop-in traffic. But one Tuesday, after working 16 days straight, I decided to take the night off, since we didn't have any reservations for the night.

I was opening a bottle of wine when the doorbell rang. A young man in his 30s was there wanting a room. I told him I was taking the night off and there was a nice B-&-B down the block. But he said my B-&-B had been recommended to him, and he really wanted to stay with me. Finally, after trying to send him away several times, I said, "Give me 20 minutes to get a room ready. "

We ended up chatting all evening. He was from the Florida Keys and had come to attend an organic foods conference.

We talked about life and our philosophies, and it was a wonderful evening. During our conversation I talked about the cabins and just before the evening ended, he said "Carol, why don't I loan you the money?"

I was aghast and said, "You don't know me from Adam. Why would you even think about such a thing?"

His reply was "I think I do know you and I'm serious."

Money Stories

Sure that morning would change his mind, I suggested we sleep on it and we headed to our rooms. But the next morning he wanted to see the property.

"Are you really sure about this? It's a considerable amount of money and I don't want to offend you but where does your money come from?"

He told me he'd just sold a business in Texas and he'd been considering putting the money in the stock market or buying other property but would rather invest in me. We decided to think about it for a week. At the end of the week I emailed him to say he was off the hook if he had changed his mind. But he hadn't!

What a spiritual gift! A guardian angel knocks on my door and I tried to turn him away! Three times!
How did the financing work out with this "angel"?

Several months went by and it was almost time to get the money. My attorney decided to request the funds early just to make sure the fellow had the money. Before my attorney called, I told her I had one request. Since there'd be four months of construction with no income, could we delay the first payment and me just pay the interest, adding the four payments to the end of the loan? My angel was fine with the request. After calling for the funds my attorney called me back. "Carol, where did you find this guy?" she asked.

"What does her question mean?" I thought. "Was this a sign the other shoe was dropping?"

My attorney's response was this: "Not only was he delaying the first payment, he had waived the interest for the four months." She asked him for clarity and he answered that yes, he was forgiving that dollar amount.

An Angel at My Door

So, long story short, the money came through with no problems. That was seven years ago. No payments have been missed and we've never met again.

So, do I believe spirituality and money work together? When it actually knocks on my door and is handed to me free? Well, not free, but certainly when there are questions about my place here at the cabins, I know I'm supposed to be here and am the steward for this effort. How could I deny that's what is supposed to be happening after this experience?

I'm sure the young man is benefitting as well. His trust in an unknown person is perhaps his lesson. But I've never let him down and I'm certainly not going to. To me, this whole experience and life are simply a question of trust.

I have to laugh. God sends help to my door and I tried to refuse it! Now how does that show my trust? That young man could have taken his gift down the block. I have to pay attention!

What a wonderful example of trusting! When did you begin your spiritual path?

I've been on a spiritual path for a long time, since a young age, and for many life times. But it was two years, at least, after I actually became a part of the Ananda group that my big lessons started. For two years I held myself back and just meditated. My feeling was that though I believed in God, my life was my responsibility.

"Stepping off the edge," so to speak became necessary as I helped put together the Palo, Alto Ananda Community. We were trying to purchase an apartment complex and needed about 5 million dollars. I was one of many investors. Some were giving more and some

Money Stories

less. I struggled and struggled with trusting these people, and was this for God or for me, and on and on.

Going back and forth with these questions brought lots of migraine headaches. What was my responsibility if I didn't contribute my exact portion and the project failed?

Finally, our minister told me not to even go there. "You need to make the decision for yourself. What you decide has nothing to do with whether this project makes it or not. If God wants it to happen, it will, with or without you."

Those words released me from the guilt and the constant questions. On the one hand I was literally giving the money to God with no attachment. On the other hand, it wasn't a donation, I was an investor, and the complex was going to benefit all of us.

In my mind, I literally gave the money to God and that was my point of stepping off the spiritual edge. My question for myself became "Was I going to walk my walk or just go through the motions?" Giving that money was a huge leap of faith and I have no regrets. Since then, I have trusted in God to provide for my needs.

Spiritual priorities are always first for me. I'm just a steward and will be provided for. My tastes are not luxurious; my place is tiny. We might say I own the cabins, but that is sort of a misnomer. Financially, everyone else owns the cabins, and I don't have any attachment to owning this property.

How did you happen to move to North Carolina? You didn't know anyone there, right?

While working at New Renaissance Bookshop, people kept coming in talking about Asheville, North Carolina. I'd never heard of it, but now it's obviously my home.

An Angel at My Door

Moving from Portland to North Carolina I had no idea what my next step was. The bookstore owner in Portland helped me with long-distance jobs, or beans and rice would still be my daily diet. After moving, I continued to work for him for a year.

There are still questions about the ultimate design and plan. At the B-&-B, there was no question. My "job" was to serve whoever walked through the door, in whatever capacity was needed, whether that was offering a bed, a good breakfast, or just comfort. And there were many occasions when, out of the blue, people would ask me spiritual questions. That happens at the cabins a little bit as well, but I still have doubts along the way and when doubts come, I pray. My answers usually come immediately.

Not long ago I was sitting here thinking "Now what, God? I'm doing this but what's the point?" No sooner had I asked that question then someone wanted to see a cabin. She felt so drawn to this area but didn't know why. And I got it. I'm here to be a catalyst, and I'm grateful.

Things to think about:
What makes you feel grateful? Make a gratitude list about the parts of your day you are grateful for just before you go to sleep. Each experience is a gift from Spirit. What can you learn from each experience? What are the lessons you've learned the most from?

As well as the beautiful, harmonious, comfortable times, I also add times that are stressful, the irritations, the times I feel guilty, and I look at what they are here to teach me. I find I learn the biggest lessons from stressful situations. The easy times are gifts as well, but they don't make as big an impact.

Money Stories

I first met **Mark Dodich** more than 25 years ago when we were both still "corporate guys." He was in sales and I was an administrative manager. We were both looking for ways to change our lives and at first we thought we could never "make it" in a non-traditional world as self-employed entrepreneurs.

Over the years we've both struggled with the notion that we could do what we love and make a living. Mark struggled at first to begin his astrological practice, and then to become comfortable, known, and trusted in this field. Now he is the local name many people think of when they want an astrology reading!

Chapter 11

Follow My Dream

"As astrologers we look at our transits and try to figure out what is going to happen. Sometimes we're really good at it, but a lot of times the universe will throw a little monkey wrench into our life and the lessons will come in from a totally different direction than we had pictured it. I'm learning to accept those experiences and love them because they keep my life fresh." Mark Dodich

Metaphysical subjects and techniques that empower spiritual growth are a source of interest for astrologer Mark Dodich. While attending Kent State University, he became fascinated with studying so-called primitive African tribes that used telepathy and healing, and even had knowledge of stars, that were not visible to the naked eye, before the telescope was invented. Mark also studied at a local spiritualist church camp, studied shamanism from Sun Bear, and developed an interest in the channeled materials of Djwahl Kuhl and Alice A. Bailey. www.astromark.us

Mark, when I say money and spirituality, what does that bring to mind for you?

Money Stories

To me, they blend well. If you are not living in a prosperous way, and let's not limit prosperity just to money, but when people go out to do the work that is their Truth, it costs money.If you are not living in a prosperous way, however you define that, you are not really tapped into what I call your *divine essence* or the God *vibration* at the level you could be.

Over the years I've watched you since you first stepped out, saying you didn't know if you were going to be able to make it just doing astrology. Now that's how you make your living. Tell me about the process of getting from then to now.

I started studying astrology in the early 1970s, mostly because some college friends were into it. From 1980 through the mid-90s I had a high-paying "suit job." I did astrology on weekends and evenings as a way to pay for classes and metaphysical books.

It was never my goal that astrology be more than a hobby. Then came a point where the corporate world just didn't work for me anymore. I was in industrial sales and that environment had a "What are you going to do for me now" kind of attitude that can burn a person out. When it came time to leave that world, it was due to philosophical differences with the entire industry and it was very evident it was time to leave.

Many teachers say, "Do what you love and the universe will support you." Who is gullible enough to believe that? But it is true. What these teachers don't tell you, though, are the gritty parts of how you have to totally reprogram yourself.

In my suit job, the base salary covered my bills and the commission was extra. Leaving that corporate job, I went to no base salary, no benefits, no paid vacations. It meant changing my way of thinking and reprogramming my thoughts about prosperity. There was no longer any illusion of a safety net.

Follow My Dream

My first four years doing this work full-time, after having done it part-time for years, were brutal. All my fears and lots of anger came up. There were lots of "the yell at God" kind of conversations. But after a while the universe just kept proving and proving that it was working for me.

For some time I'd find myself on Friday night with the rent due and nothing to cover it. I'd write a check and drop it off after 5 pm. Then, by Monday the money would be there through a gift certificate that somebody ordered or from some other completely ridiculous happening.

I'd take a part-time job while building my practice and the phone would stop ringing for readings. Then I'd quit the part-time job because it was a bad job for me and the phone would start ringing again! This happened several times; sometimes you just have to keep doing something to prove to yourself it works.

The universe showed me each time that doing my work, the phone rings, and when I try to get a part-time job to carry me through, the phone stops ringing. I finally smartened up and told myself to just trust the universe, even though my logical mind was saying "This is screwy. It won't work."

After a while, trust became more natural, and the more I trusted, the easier life got. But it's a process. It's not "Okay, do what you love and the universe will support you immediately." Well, it will, but you have to change your entire programming and the way you've been trained to think and believe.

Letting go of that programming can take time.

It took four years and it was like going through a shamanic death. I used my savings, my 401K, and started using credit cards to live on because, by God, bankruptcy was better than going back to that suit job. I had to get determined and when I got angry at the universe, the next day the phone would ring! There is something about righteous anger that works!

The logical part of me would never advise a client to go through their 401K and savings and start living on credit cards, but in my case it was necessary to get down to the core level.

Many times for me, unless I experience something, I can't talk to clients about it. I have to understand it at a really deep level.

I'm hoping that the consciousness on the planet is changing so we don't have to continue to do things the hard way. For example, you see people who get cancer and then heal themselves. Then, they go out and help others heal. My feeling is that the universe doesn't really want us to get cancer so we can help other people heal from cancer.

The same goes for prosperity consciousness. Why do we have to go through the pits of the experience to be able to teach people? Hopefully, we are reaching a place of consciousness on the planet where we can be wise and get it without having to drag ourselves through the swamp.

We are in a transition and it takes "stepping out on the edge" with trust in order to get to our destination. I think we have to show up and step out even though we don't know how it's going to happen.

That's true. Sometimes you just have to look at your intention and where your heart is. I've had to do my inner spiritual work and transform my basic belief patterns. It's just like Metaphysics 101 and the Law of Attraction say it's supposed to be.

Follow My Dream

I'm from Ohio and we had this guy named Johnny Appleseed who planted apple seeds wherever he went. My work is also about planting seeds. Some people are working with the Law of Attraction purely from the *I want more money* point of view, which is fine. I want more money too, but there's more to it than just money.

What can happen after you start learning the technique is that you learn to use those tools to be a better person, to manifest health or a better relationship, not just to get money and things. The magic comes from transforming yourself from the inside out. It's not an external thing.

I remember over the years watching you as you've gone through your transformation. The thing that really impressed me was when you bought your house.

For many people buying a house is not that big a thing, but for me, home ownership was a gigantic commitment. I heard myself saying, "Oh, my God, first, I'm committing to stay in Portland, when my intention was to move to someplace sunny. Then, who's going to do the maintenance?" which has never been my forte. I can tell a person why their soul is on planet Earth but to hang a door or do plumbing is much harder!

My life is very simple and humble now. Back in my corporate days, my suits were custom tailored in Hong Kong. Now my life is simple. It's not just the house that has changed in my life, but it's also the quality of the people and the environment I'm in. When I was playing the corporate game, everyone was trying to get something. Now the people I attract genuinely want to work on themselves and the world.

I like to joke about being the astrologer on the edge of town, like the shaman who lived outside of the

Money Stories

village. My choice was not just having a house, but of having quality people in my life, both as friends and clients. Buying the house was a much bigger decision than just buying a house.

It's interesting to me that your focus was on having to do maintenance. My focus would be on my ability to make my house payments each month and could I do that.

The payments were also a concern, but my payments were not dramatically higher than my apartment rent. My bigger fear was around maintenance. Certain things are easy to do, but for others I need to get my male ego out of the way and hire someone to do the rest.

Being able to hire someone to do things I can't is prosperity to me. For example, as a teenager, my job was to cut grass, but heaven forbid adding flowers and bushes to the yard. So I hired a gardener who loves that kind of work. She receives fair compensation and comes in once or twice a month.

My male ego used to say, "You've got to do it all yourself. You need to save that money to pay your bills." Now it's apparent that I'm also helping the gardener. She loves this work and needs the cash flow. It's a win-win situation.

A favorite story of mine about patience and prosperity has to do with divine timing. In college I desperately wanted to live in Alaska. My car was demolished in an accident and I got an old beater truck to replace it. Instead of graduating and going to Alaska, I ended up going to Houston. Houston was a boom town then. My truck would get me to sea level but not across the Rockies.

Several years later as an industrial salesman in San Francisco, my sales territory included Alaska and

Follow My Dream

the Pacific Northwest. Someone paid me to go to Alaska –my dream from nine years earlier!

Then one of my customers hired me to run their business in Alaska. That actually began my transformation from corporate guy to full-time astrologer. The company went bankrupt shortly after my arrival, but it got me to Alaska.

It's truly a sense of divine timing. In my case it took me nine years to get from Kent State to Anchorage. Of course, there were a lot of miles in between. It did happen and the dream manifested after I had given up on it.

I've had that happen for me several times working with treasure maps. I've put something on the collage that took a number of years to attract or I thought the picture represented one thing and it turned out to be another.

That's a good point. With prosperity consciousness, you have to drop your expectation of the way it's going to look when it comes to you or how it's going to come. One of my clients desperately wanted a relationship. In her chart it showed that something was coming in. You know in astrology you can't always tell how something is going look when it finally arrives.

This woman wanted to fall in love and get married and have all the relationship trappings. But her chart was more what I would call a work-related chart. Yet, she desperately wanted to be married with kids and so on.

l saw a relationship coming and told her. When she came back, it turned out that the person who came in was a mentor who helped her get promoted to a whole new level. She got the relationship, but it actually was about work and helped her do what her chart was calling her to do.

Money Stories

A lot of times I have to tell clients they need to drop expectations because it might not be like they want to picture it. It might not be as good or it could be even better.

An experience may bring up our issues. Years ago, during my corporate life back in New Jersey, I wanted to get my ministry license to start my ministry in Santa Fe. While pulling a trailer across the Midwest, my car's transmission blew. Through a series of events, Santa Fe took all of my money. My thoughts were "Oh, my God. I am doing this poor but spiritually conscious thing." It turned out that to get to Santa Fe, I had to receive financial help from my parents because of the car problems.

The last thing I wanted to do was take money from my parents and for survival reasons that's what happened. In the process my parents told me they had felt guilty not being able to help me at other times. For them, it was a blessing. So what I absolutely did not want to do turned out to be a blessing for both me and my parents.

This planet is so exceptional in the lesson department! I guess maybe being an angel and knowing what is going to happen next might be more fun but I'm always excited to see what will show up next in my life!

As astrologers, we look at our transits and try to figure out what is going to happen. Sometimes, we're really good at it, but a lot of times the universe will throw a little monkey wrench into our life and the lessons will come in from a different direction than we had pictured it. I'm learning to accept those experiences and love them because they keep my life fresh.

It can also bring up your trust issues! In my experience having left the illusion of safety and security of corporate work to do astrology full-time on my own, I

Follow My Dream

had trust issues day in and day out. But the more you do it, the easier it becomes. Also the more you do it the bigger, the lessons get! I've learned to watch what is happening in my practice, day to day, to see what is going on for me, the issues, and the answers. My issues will show up in the form of four clients coming through the door with the same questions for me to clarify. I get to see the issue from many different directions. And you know what? The four people come for readings and from somewhere deep inside, magically, the answers come!

Forgetting to have fun, take time off, and take care of myself tends to be my issue. I'm so busy doing readings and we're all busy doing our things. But I'm often saying things to clients to give me answers.

I have to block off time in my calendar to rest, which is difficult because I grew up in a "work hard" family." Part of trust, though, is that it's okay for me to play, have fun, enjoy the process, be able to take time off, *and* know the bills will get paid.

Manifesting money is not as difficult as giving me permission to be kind to myself with time off, play time, and time for relationships. Prosperity consciousness for me is more time for play, romance, and creative pursuits that don't include doing readings.

We may know what is happening with the planets but if we are not taking care of ourselves, how on earth are we going to provide the highest level of service to the people around us?

I like what you said about allowing time off for fun and play. That to me is more about abundance than money.

It's true. Once you've manifested the money for your bills, for vacation and comfort, then money becomes less motivating. Time off, friends, family, play, and creative time become more important.

Money Stories

    I'd urge people to create prosperity on all levels as long as you are going to the trouble to create it. Create it on all levels so you don't have to come back later to fill in the gaps.

Things to think about:
Do you find it is easy to take time for yourself? Do you play, vacation, take time off? Is this time of focusing on yourself allowed only after everything else is done? If you have trouble finding time for yourself, make a list of things that are fun for you. Start small by scheduling an hour or two a week or even every other week and pick something from your list that you can do in that time.

    I can easily slip into being a workaholic. Taking an afternoon out to go see a movie makes me feel refreshed and rested when I come out and ready to go back and focus on whatever I'm working on. I'm always amazed how even a short break can be the "vacation" I needed.

Money Stories

When I lived at the Oregon Coast between 1995 and 1999 I was instrumental in starting an Oregon Coast branch of Women Entrepreneurs of Oregon. I didn't realize it when I started getting the group going, but my hidden intention was to make friends. One of the first friends I made because of the group was **Quirina Kryger.**

I could always count on Quirina to be at meetings and anytime help was needed, she was the first on the scene. She knew the community and had lots of contacts. Over the years she has become one of my best friends. We have helped each other through many struggles and have witnessed each other grow into really wise women!

Chapter 12

My Highest Good

"There comes a point where peace does come and I know that whatever is happening in my life is happening for my highest good. It's not visible now, but ultimately it will become clear." Quirina Kryger

In 1991 Quirina Kryger opened Art on the Rocks in Waldport, Oregon, which combined the sale of gemstones, rocks, jewelry, and art. In 1995 Art on the Rocks was redesigned as Quirina's and her architect's interpretation of the coastal landscape, waves, and dunes. At that time the name was changed to Triad Gallery and the gallery hosted the work of local, national, and international artists. Since this interview, Quirina has sold the gallery and is now retired, but she is still an active member of the Waldport Lions and volunteers with other local organizations.

Can we talk about money and spirituality from the point of view that you have been trying to make life changes and they aren't seeming to come together? I know it's easy to see how money and spirituality flow together when things run smoothly and inside you feel you know what you're supposed to be doing. But what about when things are not falling in place? How do you see those two subjects coming together, when life is a struggle?

Money Stories

First of all, until recently there hasn't been a lack of or struggles with money. Not that I've had a whole lot, but there was no lack or the feelings that go with that. If anything, I've disregarded money. My purpose has definitely never been to make a whole lot of money, but there was always enough.

Then, a few years ago things changed. There was, all of a sudden, a lack of money. I tried to sell my house and that didn't work. Then I tried to sell the gallery, which didn't sell either. Since then I have been trying to figure out what to do next. Art is what I'm good at so I want to stay with that.

For a while it looked like the gallery had sold; then the sale fell through. The money from the gallery sale would cover the debts. I ask myself, "Is this the wrong thing to do?" But no answer comes.

How do you handle this?

I throw the *I Ching* and the *Perseverance Furthers* hexagram keeps coming up. So I persevere. Everyone gets that hexagram at times and I just need to hang in there. But hanging in there hasn't given me any results and another direction has not opened up. It's clear to me that the universe is telling me the time is not right and to keep on doing what I'm doing. But it's difficult and frustrating to be stuck.

Then, there comes a point where peace does come and I know that what is happening is for my highest good. It's not visible now, but ultimately it will become clear. Waiting is frustrating, but I still trust that whatever is happening is right for me and "why" is a stupid question. But it feels like I'm in a tunnel and can't find my way out. Usually, detachment is a way to change the energy, but even that isn't working at the moment.

My Highest Good

Do you find that when you are in that tunnel and not able to detach, that fears come up?

Yes. I've had anxiety attacks. But when the anxiety happens, I know it's just fear, and letting go of the fear is the answer. Once I let go, the fear begins to disappear, and things are okay. Now money for the first time in my life is connected with fear!

My attitude toward money used to be "screw it." Now, I ask myself, is money taking revenge on me for that attitude? There is definitely a connection with fear, and most of us seem to have fear in our lives at one point or another.

When you find yourself in those places of fear, how do you get yourself out of them?

First, by acknowledging the fear, and saying, "This is what is happening."

Then, meditating or chanting the name of God usually works for me. Chanting God's name brings me peace and helps me let go of the anxiety.

For me, when things are not easy or life is not going the way I want it to, those are the times my faith or trust are tested and most of the time it's because I'm not listening. Is this true for you? I don't necessarily get clues like "okay, here is the path and this is what you have to do." For me, peace may or may not make more money come in or an issue go away, but it makes me feel better.

That is the same with any crisis in one's life. My belief system says that if there are situations you cannot change, you can change your attitude toward them. That different focus can move me from an anxiety attack to peace.

It doesn't stop me from wondering why things aren't changing or how to get unstuck. But what does help is going back to "It must be for my highest good and somehow the reason is not visible yet."

Money Stories

Lately, I've been working with envy. Jealousy or envy have never been my issues, but both have been coming up in the past few months. These emotions shows up especially when someone else's property sells in days or weeks and mine is still sitting there.

Right now, I'm in touch with a lot of emotions that were never my problem. These emotions are coming up, and money is in that category now as well.

Did you feel before that there was a relationship between money and spirituality?

I've always felt that life is not about money. Money, to me, is not the purpose of life. Money is a man-made system, both the paper and the gold it is based on. But thinking about money takes my thoughts to value.

The value of diamonds is something our culture made up. Here on the Oregon Coast, we have agates, which I like much more than diamonds. If diamonds were on the beach, would they still be valued?

How does creativity play into your work and your life? Personally, I see creativity as a big part of spirituality.

The creative part of people is very interesting to me. I'm passionately interested in what people are creating. My gallery is about creativity and that has to do with who I show in the gallery.

I definitely support all artists and admire them for dedicating their lives to art and my gallery supports those people. Being an artist is a difficult life.

My tendency is to discriminate between those who have dedicated their lives to art instead of Sunday painters. Sunday painters usually have made their money when they were in another more lucrative field and now after retirement they get to start painting.

Working with art is what I'm meant to be doing, but it has not paid off for them or for me. Some of the

My Highest Good

my artists have been discouraged that not as much of their work sells as we'd like or as they deserve.

I could make the gallery more commercial but that can be a trap. You sell lots of commercial things, and after a while that's all you sell. It's not the direction I have chosen to go. It felt important to me to set those standards high.

Things to think about:
Are you struggling with money right now? Try making a treasure map with the focus being on abundance and flow.

What is a treasure map? It's a collage of magazine or newspaper pictures and words describing what you want to draw into your life. Your collage can be on any size or type of paper. You will need at least a half dozen magazines (and more is better) that have lots of photos and can be torn or cut up. Also, make sure the magazines have pictures that will work for your life and what you want to draw in (i.e., you don't want to have sports or computer magazines or mainly text, when you want to draw in travel or a new home or partner).

Leaf through the magazines and tear out pictures and/or words that attract your attention and fit your focus. If pictures attract your attention even though you may not know how they fit, tear them out anyway. Most of the time the picture represents something important for you that you are not yet aware of. I always put animal pictures that I'm drawn to on my treasure map because the animal's energies usually fit in some way.

Glue or tape the pictures on your paper in the way that works for you. You can even allow pictures to go outside the edges of the paper! The final thing to do before you hang the treasure map is to write *"This or*

Money Stories

something better" on the page. These words invite your guides to help you in case you have left something off or the emphasis needs to be bigger than you have made it. Hang your collage on a wall that you will see at least daily. I hang mine in the bathroom or on the wall behind my desk. Good luck!

Money Stories

I first met **Erin Donley** just after she had left her advertising sales job. She called and wanted to do an informational interview about my job. At first I wasn't going to take the time, but for some reason I was intrigued and decided to give her a few minutes. We ended up talking much longer than planned, and she became an instant friend.

We decided my job was not a good fit for her — glad of that! — but that the store might have other niches where she could be useful. Two weeks after our first contact, while she was away visiting family on the East Coast, the store all of a sudden had an opening and I left her a message to get her resume in immediately. It worked. The store owner was hooked by her resume and ended up not interviewing anyone else. Erin took a HUGE pay cut to be at the store, but through that seeming step backwards, she has made a leap of faith into who and what she was meant to be!

Chapter 13

Moving toward My Truth

"This is what spirituality is all about. Really embracing the change and learning to trust. Not just trusting my angels or trusting God or my spirit guides, but trusting myself and my capabilities. I'm totally capable of figuring it out." Erin Donley

Erin Donley is a writer, speaker, and business communications consultant and specialist in Portland, Oregon. In her business, Marketing Your Truth, and her TV show, *Reveal What's Real*, she helps "thought leaders" and New Age entrepreneurs become more believable and influential in their online and offline communications. In 2006, she left a long-time sales/marketing career in radio to serve at the spiritual hub of Portland: New Renaissance Bookshop. This helped her to merge her business savvy with those who liked the unseen and unheard things in life. Today, Erin's intention is to remind the world of the good that's created when we can speak openly about the things in life that are hidden, uncomfortable, and difficult. www.erindonley.com and www.revealwhatsreal.com.

What I wanted to talk to you about was how money works in your life or any ideas or stories you have about how mon-

Money Stories

ey and spirituality work together for you. Does money work better for you if you step into your spiritual practices?

All my life I've been well taken care of financially. As the youngest, and a girl, money was never a worry for me. Growing up we bought from Goodwill and went to the discount malls and at the same time belonged to a country club, so deprivation was never my struggle.

My college years were fortunate because my father paid for my education. He gave me money for an apartment all four years, even though I worked through high school and college. Making money and having money of my own has always been important to me, but only from jobs I liked.

After moving to Portland, I blindly landed a job selling radio commercials. Because sales was a people field, which was fun and easy for me, I learned quickly and my income reflected that. The first year my income was $25,000, then $50,000 my second year, then $65,000, and $75,000. Every year my income flowed and increased until I was making $100,000. The job was straight commission, so my income did vary, but I remember scoffing at a $3500 check because I'd thought it would be much more.

Then, the job began to feel like I was selling a piece of my soul. That's when I chose to work at New Renaissance Bookshop and my pay went from $100,000 a year to $10/hour.

I remember talking with you just after you left your radio job. Part of me could not understand why you wanted a job at New Renaissance and another part understood. What kinds of things happened to and for you during those first years at the bookstore?

Somehow, it all worked out. I knew I would be taken care of, but the reality was hard. I had to get really

Moving toward My Truth

creative. There was no way to pay my mortgage and all of my bills with my bookshop income, and the first thing I did was use up my line of credit.

This much lower-paying job became my passion and was necessary for my personal and spiritual growth. So, I immersed myself in the job, and there went the entire $25,000 home equity line of credit. I was trying to unplug from my old lifestyle, and I found that driving a Land Rover or buying $20 bottles of wine or popping into any restaurant to order a meal no longer worked.

Teaching myself new ways of living became my priority, and I was pretty resistant at first. After using the line of credit, I next cashed out my 401K. That paid off the home equity loan and left a little reserve, but soon that was being tapped, too. Then came credit cards here and there, but at first nothing too bad.

Then it hit me, I needed to figure this out or this transition would never work. That and not wanting to sell my house were what made me start my business. My house is my sanctuary and it's wonderful. I refused to give it up. And I also refused to leave the bookstore.

So my business, Marketing Your Truth, was born and it helped extend my income for about three years. During that time my spiritual practice was all about money, going back into my childhood, bringing all my subconscious money beliefs to the surface, looking at each belief to see if any were still true for me as an adult.

My workshops have been fun and I've done great with them, but issues with money just never seemed to stop. Things would get really bad, and panic would set in. Then, something always saved me at the 11th hour. That is in my astrology, that I get taken care of but always at the last minute.

Money Stories

Now, money and spirituality are hand-in-hand in every way. For the first time my paycheck is not coming from an employer. It's coming from my business, for the first time in 37 years! That brings up tons of fears. My track record for the last five years hasn't been easy or great. The shift from $100,000 to $10/hour was like starting from scratch. I'm still stubborn, and like to have a few fun things.

Where do you feel you are now? It hasn't been that long since you left the book store.

This is what spirituality is all about. Really embracing change and learning to trust. Not just trusting my angels or trusting God or my spirit guides, but trusting myself and my capabilities. I'm capable of figuring it out. Realizing that it may be a rollercoaster ride, and financially, learning to ride the wave and come to a new level of moderation is a big piece of it.

It's important to stop seeing myself as a little girl and new at this. In every one of my relationships, I was independent yet I still wanted someone to take care of me. In my current relationship, my boyfriend is financially secure and generous, and he likes my independence. He says that my financial successes are a turn-on to him. Even though he would be willing to pay for me, paying for myself is important to me. So my story of wanting someone to take care of me is not really true!

Isn't it funny how that happens? How does that fit with what you've learned at New Renaissance Bookshop?

Working at New Renaissance, there were customers who had their own businesses doing what they love but they had trouble asking for what they were worth and asking for money in general. It was shocking to see how many people did trades, and it bothered me how much suffering there was around those experiences.

Moving toward My Truth

It's important to me that people pay for my services. When people would say let's do a trade, my response was "Let's exchange the money because that energy exchange is important to the whole community." It shows that our work is a way of creation and a way of showing appreciation. At places like Burning Man, where they don't use money, it's great, but it isn't how we live in the real world. We use money. It's important to me to pay people and be able to model that behavior, and to draw in clients who value the same things. I want those I work with to learn a new level of comfort around money.

That's where the spiritual piece is for me, to see money as a way of expressing thanks and appreciation for the expertise and knowledge we bring, even if we're just getting out of the way so the universe can come through. That's fine. I want to be paid and to pay for that, and to be grateful to be a conduit.

I've heard you say you wanted to charge a little bit more than everyone else. Can you talk about that? Most practitioners say they want to charge less than everyone else. So tell me what charging more does for you.

In the beginning, it was definitely important to start with an affordable price for anyone mildly interested in hiring me. I needed to get my feet wet and gain confidence. Then, it was clear that the clients who got the most out of our work were the ones who were risk takers and were bold, feisty people with a high standard of excellence for themselves and how they communicated.

When that kind of client came to me, those qualities were in me as well, and it made me feel good. People with those values were a blast to work with and they actually appreciated that I charged a little bit more.

Money Stories

It felt a bit exclusive to them, like a challenge and they couldn't just half-way show up.

When they did come and they had paid a little more than they were comfortable with, they showed up on time, were prepared for our appointments, and wanted to gain every penny's worth from our time together. I wanted clients who would devour the insights we created together.

But even with that income from my business and New Renaissance, I still wasn't able to pay my mortgage and bills, and I was working constantly. Finally, the realization hit that it wasn't a winning combination. I was exhausted and still poor.

So with the money you make now, do you feel like you still need to figure out how to make more?

You know, this year I had the biggest shift ever, courtesy of my father who spent his whole career in the financial industry. Now he's been asked after his retirement to return as a motivational speaker. He speaks to Wells Fargo's top financial advisors about how to be real, how to connect with people and love what you do. The apple doesn't fall far from the tree!

My dad spoke in San Francisco last August and invited me to come hear him talk. All of these men and women in the audience were making tons of money and dealt with clients who made tons of money.

I left my poverty-conscious world up here in Portland and went down to the complete opposite. After spending three days hearing my dad speak, talking with all these people and seeing how some of the speakers that Wells Fargo hires bring in $5-10,000 for each event, I saw that they weren't any better than me! And they weren't any better than the people presenting at New Renaissance Bookshop. The difference was in the

Moving toward My Truth

fee, $300 to $3000 per hour as opposed to $12 per person for a talk at New Renaissance.

All of these people at this conference really care about their clients and didn't see money as dirty. They want their clients to feel free enough to talk about everything and anything that relates to their money, because really, who doesn't want financial security? To talk freely, you need someone you can totally trust. I thought people who made lots of money, especially in this industry, would be selfish and greedy, and it just wasn't true.

That weekend I realized there is no reason to doubt myself. Radio ad sales was good for me because I genuinely like people, and my biggest value is originality. And it's important to do things my way and that my work doesn't look like anyone else's.

Right now it's important for me to get advice from people I really admire and figure out what feels right for me. If it doesn't feel right, it won't work.

Do you see yourself going out on the speaker circuit?

Yes, but only if it's my way. There is a National Speakers Association and I looked into getting involved with them. But their style of marketing and networking doesn't fit my style.

Then there is this corporate circuit scene. My teachings are for executives who are highly self-reflective. Can I draw enough of an audience from that group?

If you are going to take the time to do this, you want people to get it.

I agree and I do want to make a big splash, not just a little one. Understanding what's at the heart of each person is important to me so that a real relationship can be built.

Money Stories

Back to the Speakers Association, I need to figure out if their audience works for me and how to be in front of them, and I want to charge more than $12 a person. A friend told me about an article that said the smartest people spread their income over four categories. The first category has a product. Second, getting money from services, like spending your time. Third, investments, like a house. The fourth is money from someone else, like still getting a paycheck or getting outside funding.

I thought a lot about that system and my home and my services fit two of the categories. Now, I want to start creating products that can be bought nationally and internationally, like a video workshop series. With that product I won't have to spend all of my time generating income. Who knows where the money from others will come in? Maybe, around my TV show, say someone to sponsor or fund it. Income coming in through that would be great. So right now I'm working on the four quadrants, and the product is my current focus.

Before you called this morning, I listened to a recent *Reveal What's Real* show with the four wise women. Each interview brings up so much to think about. I think sponsorship for that program would be perfect. How do you see it happening?

I know how to make it happen since I sold media ads for eight years. I know how to get in front of a business owner and present them with an opportunity that's a good match. I'd want to focus on compatible brands.

One of my radio clients was the owner of Leif's Auto Collision Center here in town. He tells you the truth that you have a choice of who fixes your car, unlike what many insurance companies may tell you.

My TV show is about personal growth and these heart topics. My first thought was he'd never be inter-

Moving toward My Truth

ested, but since he's a "truth sayer," he might love it.
Of all the commercials I see and hear, he seems like someone who might be interested in sponsoring you.

We clicked back then, but fear tells me he'll say "No." He's like the Donald Trump of Portland. People walk on tippy-toes around him because he's brilliant. It wasn't scary to be sitting and asking for thousands of dollars for the radio station, but asking for $500 for something I really believe in is really difficult.

Is the fear you sometimes feel because you are no longer working for someone else? Getting out there with our own message and products can be really difficult. When you work for someone else you step out not as yourself but as that other business. Being self-employed, you step out there as yourself. That, to me, is one of the scariest things I can do.

Actually, it is scarier for me to think about representing someone else's business right now. The fact was that I was a company talking to a company, not the person Erin Donley, and people treated me like that. That was never comfortable for me. I cared so much about whether these advertisers got what they paid for. I could talk to them about having the right amount of commercials on the right station, but not whether the message was right. If I did, they'd say, "You're just a sales person. You don't know who my audience is." Or my boss told me it was not my place to have those conversations.

That is another reason I started Marketing Your Truth – to help people fine-tune their message so that it brings in the customers they really want. That was the missing piece when I was working in advertising. How many crappy radio commercials do you hear everyday? The crappy ones also seem to be the ones that play over and over and over again. Great commercials do great

Money Stories

things, but even the bad commercials if played often enough can be memorable and somewhat effective.

The word *thanks* keeps coming to mind. I'm so grateful for the money that is coming in. The people I'm working with now are great and I'm so much more comfortable receiving their money.

An example of a change in me is that my mother loaned me money to buy my car and I arranged to send her $200 each month to pay off the loan. She did it to help me through a money crisis and didn't charge me interest.

A couple of months ago when I began to look at leaving the book store, panic came up. Mom told me to take a break from paying her. I ended up asking for several extensions, but it felt so bad every month I didn't pay her. I felt like that little girl again. In some ways it seemed crazy to me because she didn't need that $200.
But whether she needed it or not is not the point! It's your deal, not hers.

You are so right! I thought "What is the spiritual part of this? What if this was reframed and every time I wrote her a check, it was a check to my success?" It's an investment in me and my ability to be fully adult. So I sat down and wrote out the remaining checks to my mom. I put them in the mail and did a little ceremony.

Every time I do something like look at my bank account or get a little scared and then figure out what to do next, my rewards come. A new client will show up or a random paycheck comes in. That's kind of my spirituality from the universe or God, saying "Okay, listen, you take a look at every hard truth around this, and we will reward you."
When you are really aware of what you are doing and not just doing it mindlessly, and you get in that spiritual place with money, then not only does it hit your first chakra, but

Moving toward My Truth

it also hits your crown chakra as well. Maybe what it does is open up all of the chakras rather than just hitting the first one. I've never thought about it that way. But I think it's a big spiritual piece.

That's such a great point. Like heaven and earth coming together. It's brilliant. I like that.

Who do you look up to or who do you want to be like?

My father. He has such a healthy relationship with money and he's so generous with it. He's bailed me out several times, but not in ways that take away my power. I still have a little of this belief that it's not possible to be yourself, say what you need to say, be absolutely genuine and honest, and still make a comfortable amount of money. And if a compromise is needed, it has to be the money.

For so long now I studied what to say, and how to say it. But every once in a while it fails miserably. Then it's two steps back. With a failure I get shaken and find myself moving backwards. From that backwards movement, I think I can't be successful as myself. That is my biggest core issue right now. So, I need to help myself first and then I can help others, which I'm committed to on a daily basis.

Things to Think About:

Who has been your mentor? What have you learned from your mentor? How has knowing her or him changed who you have become? Is there someone in your life who needs a mentor? Can you step out and help them without taking away their power? Are you already a mentor? What are you teaching? What are you learning and receiving back from this exchange?

I've always found that I've gained more from being a mentor than I've ever given, because I teach what I need to learn. Have you found this to be true?

Stories about Dharma

Money Stories

I met **Stan Madson** around 1997 at my first International New Age Trade Show in Denver. I was at a party held by Llewellyn Publishing and I felt intimidated by all of the famous authors in the room. Stan's table had a few empty seats, and I asked if I could join him, and we began to chat. When he told me he was co-owner of the famous Bodhi Tree Book Store in Hollywood, California, I would have been even more intimidated except for Stan's graciousness.

We became friends that night, and over the years we met at book shows for lunch or dinner, or just to sit and chat about books and what was happening for independent book stores. The two times Book Expo America was held in Los Angeles, Stan and Bodhi Tree's co-owner, Phil Thompson, hosted a dinner for a few book people and gave us a guided tour of their store. Stan is exceedingly unselfish with his time and in sharing his knowledge about books and authors. I thank him for his generosity with this interview.

Chapter 14

Right Livelihood

"I guess I would answer your question more from a right livelihood point of view. If you are involved in something that you find is intrinsically warming to your entire being, something that feels good, that you don't have reservations about its merit, and you feel it is worthwhile, then that, to me, is the direction of spirituality. In a sense it embraces everything." Stan Madson

For more than 41 years, Stan Madson was co-owner, with Phil Thompson, of Bodhi Tree Book Store in Hollywood. The shop was a staple in the metaphysical arena. In 1983 Shirley Maclaine made the book store famous in her book *Out on a Limb* (although both Stan and Phil say the actual incident of the book falling off the shelf onto her happened at another area book store). Late in 2011, after more than four decades in business together, Stan and Phil sold the book store property on Melrose Avenue and closed the store. In May of 2012 the store assets were sold and the new owner plans to open an expanded version of Bodhi Tree in late 2013.

How do money and spirituality relate for you, or do they?
Money and spirituality? Well, I suspect that they do relate to each other to some degree. To me they re-

Money Stories

late in the sense that a measure of whether or not you are reaching out and being successful, say as book store owners, is whether or not what you stock, how you present it, and who you are as an identity comes back to you in the form of customers and sales or people buying what you have. Or they sign up for your seminars, presentations, and readings. So, that can be related to money flow.

If that flow is stifled, then customers aren't being reached. But if what you are expressing is sufficiently meaningful to a number of people, then the money flows back to you. As far as a relationship between money and spirituality being absolutely necessary, that has not been part of our way of thinking at Bodhi Tree.

Phil's and my goal for the store hasn't been with the intention of success or looking to become millionaires or anything of that sort. Our intent was not from a money point of view. It was always about service, quality, and completeness. With that in mind, our view of success was always that we would be supported in some kind of reasonable sense. That was our view of success.
So, in your personal life do you see any connection between money and spirituality? Or how do you see either of these working for you or not?

I can't say I've thought of it that way or put those two together. I guess my answer would be more from a right livelihood point of view. If you are involved in something that you find is intrinsically warming to your entire being, something that feels good, that you don't have reservations about its merit, and you feel it is worthwhile, then that, to me, is the direction of spirituality. In a sense it embraces everything.

Being eclectic is what we, at Bodhi Tree, have done best, and what I have done, personally. We were

Right Livelihood

talking about Esalen recently; the idea of a religion of no religion is a catch phrase that feels right for what we have done all these years. You draw on everything and look for an intuitive recognition that it has value and good energy. If that works, then that's enough. And the fact that there has been an adequate life-style coming out of it is all well and good. If that financial support wasn't there, I expect that we'd have scrambled around and looked for something different that would have given more monetary returns.

The idea of right livelihood, to me, is another way of speaking about spirituality.

Right livelihood is almost like no matter what you are doing, if it gives you energy and is warming to you, no matter what it is, that makes it powerful in its own sense. There are traditional stories about the powerful Zen Roshi who is paddling his boat across the river taking passengers back and forth. People asked him how he could do such a mundane thing. He says that each trip across the river is unique in itself, and this is a great approach for life.

I know that you and Phil are in your right livelihood. Do you want to say a few words about how the two of you started Bodhi Tree?

You've probably heard the story before. All of us who started the store were aerospace engineers. It was a time of political and social upheaval, much like right now. There was an unpopular war and our work complex made products that supported the war. We all had personal and inherent problems with the products we worked on and decided that we didn't want to continue to be part of the war effort.

It was also a time when there was new music being introduced, as well as the psychedelics and the

Money Stories

hippie movement. People were stimulated to make spiritual journeys to the East. From those journeys people like Ram Dass came back with interesting stories and new ways of looking at their lives, and the world. The Maharishi launched Transcendental Meditation, which appealed to us a great deal. Plus, we got involved with Krishnamurti and his teachings to some degree.

We asked ourselves what other work we could do and what we were interested in. Arts and crafts and books were our interests at that time. So we tried to design a way of working that would interest and delight us, and the book store was born.

At first, only a few of us could work at the book store, and the rest would have to continue their old jobs for a while. But the eclectic mix that the store offered immediately began to grow and become popular. Within a year we were all, including our wives, working full time at the store. From the beginning, the store has been something that drew lots of all kinds of people.

Our customers gave us direction when they asked us to get this or that, and from them we knew what our next step was and what line of products or books we should get that would bring people into the store. We constantly took any and all revenues and revolved them back into the store to create the environment. We've done that since the beginning.

In later years, we didn't have as much chance to listen as in the beginning. We tended to get information so quickly from computers and the web that we were hardly ever surprised. But, occasionally, we still did get unusual information, and we would run out and find those new product lines. Eckhardt Tolle is an example. We heard about him from Kolin Lymworth at Banyon

Right Livelihood

Tree Books up in Vancouver, BC, a year before we finally acted on the information.

Did you see *The Secret* and *What the Bleep Do We Know?!* as examples of those ideas?

Yes. At first *The Secret* was an idea that we had a hard time figuring out. It took a couple of months before we finally figured it out; then, it took another couple of months before we were able to get copies of the DVD stocked in the store. *The One* was a similar DVD that some of our customers liked better.

When I worked at the Bookshop, *What the Bleep Do We Know!?* was huge for us but not in the beginning. Flyers were dropped off at the store, and at first that funny name didn't resonate as a spiritual model. But then, the owner of Beyond Words Publishing in Hillsboro, Oregon said "GO SEE IT!" When we did we knew it would be big.

We had the same experience. After we watched the DVD, we realized that it had big potential. There was a lot of peripheral material, like the books and DVDs of the authors interviewed in the movie. So we put together book lists and reference materials and displays to make it easy for customers to find the information from both *What the Bleep Do We Know!?* and *Down the Rabbit Hole.* People would come in and say things like "There was this woman in *What the Bleep...* Do you know who I'm talking about?"and we could take customers right over to the shelf where that material was and hand them the book. It was big!

For us *What the Bleep Do We Know!?* had a lot more importance than *The Secret* because it launched the notion of how science and the metaphysical world can be combined. There were not a lot of people who understood how close the two subjects are.

Increasingly, I think the scientific role will have a stronger relationship to the spiritual world. The quan-

Money Stories

tum approach to spirituality is one that still has growth left. It's interesting that people, through *What the Bleep Do We Know!?*, get a strong sense of how their fundamental being vibrates with the entire cosmos.

The people behind *What the Bleep Do We Know!?* were able to popularize it enough that people became warm to the ideas. Now customers are going back and looking at all these other basic books and ideas, like Capra's *Tao of Physics*. It's so great!

Paris Hilton was famous for coming into your store to buy books before she went to jail a few years back.

I'm not sure she got *The Secret* here. She did come in and that was just a couple of weeks before she went to jail. There was a line of photographers taking pictures of her through the front window. The books she got from us were John-Roger's *Spiritual Warrior* and Eckhart Tolle's *The Power of Now*.

Much of the publicity around Paris Hilton was very rude and snide: a person like her getting involved with that material just to make a splash! However, from a book store point of view we have always found that this sense of becoming a spiritual person can strike at any time. You never know quite what will make it happen for any particular person. It doesn't have to be a big deal to make it happen.

We have found that we can't even be cynical about "simple" books because many of those have changed people's lives as well. Here is Paris Hilton, a person who had no real relationship to the spiritual community, getting some of the seeds planted. All I can say is that it's a wonderful opportunity for her. It's a shame those commentators didn't see it that way.

Right Livelihood

Things to think about:
Right livelihood is a concept that has to do with meaning and a sense of purpose connected with one's work. We all may have it at times, but some people have it most or all of the time. Do you? What would right livelihood look like in your life? What things give you a sense of meaning and a sense that your work makes your life worthwhile? What would you change if you had the opportunity? What would it take to make right livelihood happen for you?

Most of my jobs have had some sense of right livelihood for me, though some had more than others. My favorite job and the one that felt more like I was in the spiritually right job for me was my event job at New Renaissance. At the book store I learned to meditate regularly and to speak up for myself, and I got to meet many fascinating people. New Renaissance was built on spiritual principles, and I got a chance to see those principles in action. I worked with the book store for nearly 15 years and had the opportunity to work through some of my personal issues and struggles. Though this job was my right livelihood, it was not sweetness and light all the time. I worked harder than I had at any other job. But I felt more in touch with my spirituality at this job than at any before that point.

Money Stories

demystifying Medical Intuition, brought Lori Wilson to Portland to do a book talk and signing. We had an instant connection. I had spent several years studying Caroline Myss's work and the idea of medical intuition fascinated me. A medical intuitive can scan your body for illnesses and places that are out of balance or headed toward illness, and Lori, has been doing this this kind of work for many years.

    I was so curious about medical intuition and how one could make a living doing it that after talking with Lori I asked her if she'd allow me to interview her. By the time we reconnected it had been a while since we had talked, but getting back in touch to check facts of her story brought back our instant connection.

Chapter 15

More than Just Affirmations

"I think money is necessary to insure the security of your vision." Lori Wilson

Lori Wilson, BA, MSW, founder of Inner Access 101, is a social worker, author, weekly radio show host, trainer, and medical intuitive. She specializes in channeling, regression, medical intuition, and business intuition, and has been in private practice for over 30 years. Demand outweighed her time and ability so Lori created a strong network of practitioners and trainers who can offer many of the same specialized services she offers. A visionary and self-professed "mother bear," Lori's passion to spread inner trust is evident in all she does. Her mission is to encourage as many people as possible to trust themselves first. Lori is the author of *demystifying Medical Intuition.* www.meetloriwilson.com

What's an experience or memory you have about money?
One of my earliest money experiences was babysitting when I was young. With that babysitting money I'd to treat my friends to whatever we could buy. Back then you could buy an entire huge bag of chips for 25 cents and my pay for babysitting was 50 cents an hour.

As I got a little bit older, we went to dances at our church. We found that if I paid for my ticket to get

Money Stories

in, then if we licked our hands properly, we could actually get the ink to smear on three other's hands to get them into the dance, too. It wasn't a particularly honest thing to do, but we had a good time for a small bit of money. And I was able to splurge on my friends.

When do you remember being able to put together the ideas of money and spirituality?

I realized early in the 1980s, at the beginning of my career, that there was a lot of confusion regarding this concept. Many people thought that if something was spiritual work, say doing healings, you weren't supposed to ask for money for it. That idea never made sense to me. My work is time, time spent training or developing my skills and my career. My work as an intuitive or as a counselor is my job. And of course, I should get paid for that work.

So your view is that if work has a spiritual connection the person should still get paid for it? It's my point-of-view as well.

Absolutely! Not getting paid for the work is like saying that you shouldn't charge for bread in the store because it's bread and everyone eats it. It doesn't make sense how people have confused offering spiritual services as something you shouldn't get paid for.

What messages did you get from your family about money?

Well, we didn't have a lot of money when I was growing up. So, the messages from my family were that it's hard to keep money, there's not enough, and you have to give yours away: my dad borrowed a lot of money from us kids and we just gave it to him.

How have your ideas about money changed since childhood?

I think money is necessary to insure the security of your vision. Right now I require a fair bit of money to do what I want to do professionally and money is a

More than Just Affirmations

vehicle to carry out my mission. Some people may need more money than others depending on what their mission is.

I've worked with people since 1981 as an educator, a counselor, and an intuitive practitioner. I have tons of resources and information about people's beliefs about money, their experience about money, growing a business, and people's reactions to money.

To date, I've trained more than 4500 students in intuition, channeling, and medical intuition, which is all considered healing and spiritual work. Working with money and marketing are part of our *Channeling as a Profession* and *Medical Intuition* courses. I feel it's necessary to teach students the importance of valuing their services financially. I don't want to just send them out the door to find their own way.

Making what you love work as a career versus being able to do the work are entirely different skill sets. Marketing and promoting their work is where a lot of healers, intuitives, and even good counselors fall down. A huge piece of any successful business or private practice is about money, of feeling worthy to ask for money, of knowing how to put a price tag on your work.

The biggest challenge many of my students have with money is that they love what they do, but they don't know how to charge for it. That's where a lot of my students get things confused between spirituality and money.

My training was first as a counselor and social worker so I always expected to be paid for my work. As I added more intuitive skills over the years, I already knew that I should be paid for my time and expertise. The expertise might have changed, but it was still my career. I've always considered what I do to be my career.

Money Stories

That change in expertise is where lots of people have problems. If they have worked in another helping field, say as a nurse or whatever, they are used to being paid by the hospital, but then adding Reiki to their skill set, for example, they may not know how to structure their fees for this new piece. They love their work and are spending time with people, so they may not think they should charge for this new service they now provide.

Another thing is working for yourself versus working for an organization or agency. They might say, "Now, that I'm working for myself, how do I charge for these services?"

That is huge! Over the years, for the students I've trained, that's a huge challenge. As I mentioned earlier, it isn't the skills they struggle with, it's packaging the skills, marketing them, feeling comfortable considering their work a career. Especially if some of it is not traditionally credentialed.

It is about valuing yourself and your time and how you package your work and yourself.

A pet peeve of mine is relying on affirmations. The use of positive affirmations was popular in the 1980s and 90s, and still is. Many people believed that if you say a positive affirmation ten times and if you believe it for half a minute, the money is going to come flowing to your door. That's just not reality.

Of course, you do need to think positively, but you need to do a little more as well.

I tell my students, "Having the skills and being a good person are not going to make your business work. You have to keep at it, and market it. About 30% of your time, even in a casual private practice, is about marketing." To do this work for a living you always need to make sure that you are marketing. You have to create

More than Just Affirmations

the work and then deliver your services. It's not good enough just to be able to provide the service. We'd all love that. I'd love it, too, but truly it is not enough.

Do you teach marketing in all of your classes?

In the *Channeling as a Profession*, *Regression Training*, and *Medical Intuition* classes, but not the Access Intuition 101 class because the focus is beginning students or those picking up additional skills. In classes where we are measuring and putting our endorsement on students, the skills and how to market go hand-in-hand. I can't teach people a skill set and then not teach them how to make a business out of the skills.

Some believe if they say a positive little quote, then things will be given to them. It doesn't work that way. Saying an affirmation and being a positive person isn't anywhere near enough to insure financial or business success in a spiritual field. It might be one percent on a good day of why you succeed. I wish the easy way were true, but I'm a realist.

Even best-selling authors and healers need marketing.

Of course they do. They didn't just wake up and become an overnight success. Many people have said to me, "This is amazing what you do. You are so lucky." Luck has nothing to do with it. Gutting it out, working on marketing, working hard, and having staying power have all been necessary for me. I absolutely love what I do for a living and fortunately, I have also learned to love the marketing part. The only part I do not love so much is the accounting – but I have become very good at that part too!

How long have you had your own business?

I've been in private practice my entire career, since 1983. I'm the sole supporter of my family and

Money Stories

have two very large businesses. I tell people that doing what you love is possible.

How long did it take you to make a living with your business?

Looking back at the beginning, it probably took me about three years. These days some people might be able do it in less time with applied effort. If you are building a sustainable career, it is realistic to plan on taking 2-5 years before you can relax enough to be comfortable about where the next bag of groceries will come from. I am still fairly certain that the least time it would take would be a good solid year and a half to make a presence for yourself.

You've got to have some target niche ideas, too. You can't just put out a business card and hope people will find you. You need to change, and keep your profile in different areas of the community, and have fun. Part of spirituality and money is making sure you price yourself accordingly. If you net 40 to 50 cents on the dollar after taxes and expenses, that's good. It's a little bit of a reality check.

I won't pretend for a minute that it's been easy for me. Anyone who has done what they love and has been successful beyond their own family's needs can say that. I've never met anyone who said it was easy. Have you ever met a business owner who says it was easy? It costs a lot of money to grow a business.

How long have you had your school?

We don't actually refer to Inner Access 101 as a school. We started teaching classes in 1994. I have purposefully chosen a business model for what you are calling a school so that we could be nimble and flexible as well as keep the standards very strong for the work we do.

More than Just Affirmations

Getting my book, *de-mystifying Medical Intuition* out there has helped. With the company, the book, our trainers, and our graduates, there are a lot of good people who deliver high-caliber services. There are enough people trained that can provide our style of body scans all over the world.

Can you tell me more about the medical intuition program?

People wanting to get trained in the medical intuition work undertake a year to a year and a half program. Besides the 12 days of course work, they also have to do 18 unpaid body scans within a year, with their trainer checking their scanning skills, and they need to write two papers. It is a fair commitment.

We could teach a thousand people in a big hall how to do medical intuition, but to be certified they all have to do the 18 scans. Each scan takes an hour or more of their time, and an hour of the trainer's time to mark. Time becomes a real issue in certifying masses. While we could teach a thousand, our company can certify only 80-100 within any given year.

One year I had 70 students and in the end 56 were certified, I marked over 1200 scans that year. That's a lot of time spent checking students, at an hour or more per scan! It is my chosen way to make sure that if somebody says they can do our style of scans, we can stand behind them with our reputation. We acknowledge that they learned the work and can do a scan the way we taught them, but we are not a licensing body and we don't monitor them after they walk out the door.

Financially, it would be fabulous to be teaching thousands of people these skills each year. But to be ethical and clear to the public, we have to be comfortable with our standards for certification in a very subjective field. We currently have six trainers, which you may

Money Stories

think would be a challenge because you have six different personalities marking the scans. But our standard and marking protocol is very tight, very mathematical. The score sheets the trainers fill out are pretty extensive.

What about the channeling work you do. How does that work financially?

When I started channeling Grandmother, my ancient Shoshone spirit guide, I got a lot of feedback from the native and non-native communities that a white person shouldn't be making money and using their native traditions for profit. It was challenging to know how to handle other people's perceptions about spirituality. But Grandmother's bottom line was "We are not trading counsel for food or help any longer. If there was a native person channeling a white guide, do you think there would be a problem?"

In the first five years that I did the channeling, I received about 40 complaints or pieces of hate mail. I handled them all, but it was sad for me to be bringing my work forward and doing what my guide asked and receiving that kind of resistance. This work should be respected. No culture has the corner on spirituality. I have dedicated my entire career to helping people connect with greater realms and sources of wisdom. I cannot create curriculum or support my family on volunteer work.

Let's revisit affirmations. Is there anything positive that can be gained using affirmations?

I don't say you shouldn't do affirmations. Just don't count on them as the *only* thing to make your business work. Affirmations alone aren't enough. We might not like math or money, but we wouldn't mind if someone else collected the money or told us how much to charge. The asking piece can be hard at first, setting it

More than Just Affirmations

up, deciding how much to charge, paying the bills, and managing the accounting. People can be turned off by it, but it's a part of business, and of life.

I think it's like any creative field. Look at writing. Most new authors don't think about marketing when they write a book and marketing is so important in getting the word out about their product.

They don't know about all the steps and the hard work that it takes to actually make a book sell. How do you get your potential clients and readers to come to you? People think that because there are book stores to sell books, that writing is all they have to do. But how do you get your book in the store, and then how do you drive people to the store to find your book? Or how do you drive them to pick up the phone to call for an appointment? It's all part of the structure to build a successful business. If I'm good and I provide a good service, that is only part of making a business work.

Things to think about:

Do you want to change your life? Do you know what changes you want to make? Can you voice your visions? I have found that until I can voice my visions, say them out loud or have a picture in my mind of what they will look like, I can't make the leap. Once I can at least somewhat see what the next step will look like or tell someone else what I want, then I can begin to take the necessary steps toward these visions. I also have to remember that sometimes when my vision is not clear, it's because I'm not ready to take the steps needed to make the change.

Lori also suggested that we do the following: Make a list of all the steps and follow through with them. Re-evaluate yearly. Have staying power. And of course – market, market, market!

Money Stories

One day when I was working at New Renaissance Bookshop, **Jacqueline Mandell** came into the store and called me over. She held a copy of that month's *O Magazine* and was pointing to a picture of two teenaged girls. "Guess who this is," she said and covered the picture's caption. When I said I didn't know she showed me that it was a picture of her dressed in Buddhist Nun garb.

    She had been on a pilgrimage to India and had no idea how the magazine had gotten the photo. But the picture showed me how long Jacqueline had been on her spiritual path and how important it was to her. This is her story about how she has been able to bring spirituality into her everyday life.

Chapter 16

The Mindfulness of Money

"My relationship to my finances is pretty transparent. It's not heavy or loaded for me anymore. This attitude did not come spontaneously. It came from knowing the quality of equanimity or calmness of mind. And of course, mindfulness and paying attention." Jacqueline Mandell

Jacqueline Mandell has been a student of Buddhist meditation for many years and has been on pilgrimages to Central Tibet, India, Burma, Thailand, and Japan. She teaches Tibetan Buddhist meditation and is authorized to teach in three Buddhist lineages. Weekdays, Jacqueline works for a financial institution. In both of her roles, Jacqueline offers a wide range of skills while listening intently to each person's experiences and needs. www.samdenling.org

You are a spiritual teacher. How does working at a financial institution blend with your spirituality?

I get to stay present and apply basic skills to both. Working with people and their money requires listening and paying attention, and meditation requires the same. Also, there's the intentionality of kindness, helping, and serving people with my skills.

Money Stories

The Buddhist spiritual path teaches kindness, compassion, and helping people. In terms of working at a financial institution, the goal is helping people with their money. My job is about helping people understand what's happening with their money, and I'm able to communicate about money in a calm and patient way. I educate people, and my patience, calmness, and tone of voice allow each person to understand and solve their problems. I need to have a kind of modulating sensitivity. It's like moment-to-moment meditation because each moment is changing and each person is so different.

I remember back when you were unemployed for a year. You always seemed so calm and peaceful during that year.

That was a few years back. The previous financial institution I worked for closed because the parent company went bankrupt. Everyone was laid off. I had worked for them for three and a half years and was out of work for a year. It was an interesting time.

I found my present job in the newspaper. The ad asked for a caring, passionate person to work full-time weekdays at a financial institution. It was amazing to see those words voiced in the ad along with "you will be able to offer financial power and direction." At the interview I felt totally comfortable and getting this job was a real opportunity. We have the chance to attend trainings such as being our best at work and bringing our best each day. Amazing!

There is a kind of forward movement with this job. I come home invigorated, rarely tired, and I feel in harmony, spiritually. I can be straightforward and helpful and can apply the compassionate skills of Buddhism. I don't sit there and meditate, but I do sit there fully present. There is encouragement in the work en-

The Mindfullness of Money

vironment that supports our using these qualities. The institution's mission promotes service, and our wishing to provide quality service for customers comes across.

The Dalai Lama says that our happiness is based on the happiness that we offer to others. Helping people solve a problem or find clarity around a money issue brings a lot of happiness and peace.

Tibetan Buddhism has a certain wealth practice. In that tradition, wealth means wealth of dharma and it refers to financial and personal wealth that is meant to help others.

A few years ago a couple of us went to hear musician-activist Bono speak. He is quite involved in eradicating the AIDS epidemic in third-world countries, as well as debt in African countries. After studying economics at Harvard, Bono believes African debt relief would be beneficial to our country and others. He said a number of researchers are looking at this topic.

It's interesting how societies have evolved. At one time the earth provided everything and then we decided to trade differently and money became symbolic of what we traded. We used to trade food and other goods and could usually provide for ourselves. Then there was a shift and money became collateral and people began to feel like they didn't have enough collateral. That feeling of lack impacted their self-esteem, and so forth. Hearing Bono speak, I see that we all need to work together and cooperate. Money in our society is about trade and stability, and it is what we all need in order to have a quality life. Whether eradicating AIDS or having a safer environment, both are about common goals.

Did you grow up with those kinds of attitudes about money?

Money Stories

Noooo! My daughters are much more knowledgeable about money than I was at their ages. They work and make money and know what it is. Growing up I didn't have the understanding of what money was or how hard some people had to work to earn it. I was aware that everything cost money, but I wasn't taught to embrace generosity and straight-forwardness about money. My present focus is to embrace positive qualities any time I talk about money. That's not at all how I was raised.

I feel so much more free around money because I talk about it all day long. I want to put forward the qualities of a positive attitude, clarity, and stability, and my medium just happens to be money.

Did the last place you worked for have the same values about money?

They were very straightforward, but they had time limits on everything. When there is a time limit the opportunity to help people is not as available. It's a very different feeling, relating to someone while we have a conversation. Without a time limit, conversations about money and spiritual qualities have time to come through. But if you just have time to answer a question and then it's on to the next call, that does make it more difficult. You can be honest and straightforward but then there is a time pressure.

I now work with very nice people who have been at their jobs a long time. They get along fabulously. When the spirit is good between co-workers, that has an amazing impact on an institution. It gets communicated, and everyone feels it.

Is there anything else you want to say about money and spirituality?

The Mindfullness of Money

What I've learned doing this work and having money talks with people is that it's not easy for some people to talk about money. For me, it's really easy to just sit down and have a financial conversation with anyone. It is worthwhile letting people know that these kinds of conversations are possible.

In our society people fight about money. Many times it is an obstacle or a secret. But it can be a very open topic since the exchange of money is the basis of so many things. In some ways since it is integrated so much into my life, it's hard for me to say what is spiritual and what is not with regard to money. On a daily basis, I bring an attitude from my morning meditation of really wanting to help people. That gives me the motivation to just listen, and to increase my financial skills so I can be of service.

Is that what your idea of spirituality is all about?

For whatever Karmic reasons, I have wound up working with money. It's all about simplicity because numbers are numbers. How you choose to use your money or to save it or keep track of it is what I'm talking about. My relationship to my finances is pretty transparent. It's not heavy or loaded for me anymore. This attitude did not come spontaneously. It came from knowing the quality of equanimity or calmness of mind. And, of course, mindfulness and paying attention. That's the place it started. Then, acquiring the financial skills I needed and being able to solve problems or make constructive suggestions. When I talk about financial information, it is paired with the "long enduring mind" (about duration and timing) in conversation.

Keys from a Buddhist point of view are non-greed, non-grasping, and selflessness. If people are relating to money as "I need more than my neighbors or

Money Stories

friends have," it's an attitude of a solidified self. It's also an attitude of greed and holding on. Buddhism is about generosity, letting go, and serving others.

When I help someone solve a problem, it helps me, too, and I feel more open. I guess in terms of spirituality, I have a spiritual experience. That really impacts me and it probably impacts others, too. They are left knowing it's safe to have these conversations.

Things to think about:
Buddhism teaches that money is not evil. How we deal with money is the important thing. What do you believe about money, that it's good, neutral, or evil? These beliefs can be hidden and we might think we believe one way but carry messages from childhood that are different. If you are having trouble manifesting money, internalized childhood messages could be your problem.

One of my new practices (because I still carry a few beliefs passed on from my parents) is to send my money positive energy. I can hold it in my hands when I meditate or send it Reiki. If you don't know Reiki, take a folded bill in your hands and send it love. Try starting your day this way for a month and see how the flow changes.

Money Stories

Joanne McCall was the publicist for author Kay Allenbaugh, who came to New Renaissance Bookshop in 1998 to talk about her book, *Chocolate for a Woman's Heart and Soul*. Joanne set up the event and escorted Kay to it. That night Joanne and I got a chance to talk and I felt a kinship with her. A few months later Joanne came to see me. She wanted to give a talk about publicity for customers' books and products. That first talk was a sell-out and soon became a longer workshop that was always well attended.

Joanne and I have had coffee and a chat a couple of times a year since then to talk about what is new in our lives. Our work and its focus have changed dramatically over the years and I love our times together. Joanne always has wonderful tidbits to share that I can add to my practice immediately (see the end of this chapter for one such practice).

Chapter 17

Knowing What You Want

"I tell people to stand in their power. Knowing what you want is so critical in having a vision. If you focus on how you can give and help others instead of falling into your fear, step by step, day by day, you will accomplish what you want. You will get there!" Joanne McCall

At 16, Joanne McCall wrote, directed, and performed a hometown radio show. After college, she worked as a newscaster, interviewer, and radio host in Wisconsin, Minnesota, Illinois, Iowa, and finally Oregon, where she was hired as PR Director and Special Events Planner, organizing PR and handling thousand-people events for such giants as Deepak Chopra, Marianne Williamson, and Kenny Loggins. After two years, Joanne started her own publicity firm, which beautifully integrates her love for the pace and personalities of the media, her skills with listening to and understanding clients' needs, and her ability to ignite excitement and buzz with the public. Now she creates programs and trainings to help others promote their own books and services. www.joannemccall.net; www.mediapolisher.com

Can you say something about how you bring spirituality into your business?

Money Stories

In workshops, teleseminars, and webinars I talk a lot about bringing spirituality into business, sometimes directly and other times not quite so directly. It depends on the client. Some are ready to hear this; others aren't ready yet. However, one thing I do know is that each of us has a message to bring to the world. Some people are clearer about their message. Others are still looking for it. Even those who know what their message is still may have hurdles to climb. Those hurdles are releasing what blocks them from being able to speak their message clearly, out in the world. We all need to be able to speak our message clearly, without shame or letting less-than-helpful childhood messages get in the way.

Maybe a parent or teacher told you to "quit bragging. Settle down. Quit being a show off." I think all of us got some of those negative thoughts. We need to be able to stand up with our message and not let anything get in the way. For some of us, a lot needs to be cleared out. Once that happens, we can step forward and speak our truth and begin our journey. To me, that is a spiritual process.

We need to be able to talk about what we do in a free, clear, engaging way, so people can hear us. That's how I open my events, whether they're virtual or on the ground. I offer tools and techniques for standing in your truth and being able to speak up. These tools are quite powerful. For those who need more work regarding childhood issues holding them back, a counselor or therapist might be needed.

So your work is about helping people stand in their power, say who they are and what they are here to do, and to help them be able to speak that out to the world?

Exactly! It may be that you have written a book or have a tape series or you offer classes. Whatever it

Knowing What You Want

is, once the path is clear for you to speak that message, anyone who hears it will get it. Being clear allows the flow from the universe. When you feel really inspired by someone, you want to purchase their book or listen to their message. When you are being authentic, people just know. If your message is not clear, people know that, too. I help people with publicity for their product and that begins with them first getting very clear.

How is what you teach different from, say, Coca Cola or IBM or McDonald's publicity? Is there a difference between what you teach and promotions from some of the big multinational companies?

Obviously, there are many companies that are money-driven and they have money to put behind advertising and hiring a whole department dedicated to PR. There are many individuals in these organizations who are heart-driven and believe in what they are doing. They have an impact on the organization as a whole. It's an intangible thing.

I know there are wonderful people working for big companies. The organization may be a dry, heartless thing, with a single intention of bringing in money and in the world of big corporations it's a whole different game and a different level of consciousness. In a heart-driven business, you attract the people you need to be part of your team and to help you do what it is you need to do.

We are both self-employed. How is that different from working for a corporation?

A lot of people reading this will either have worked for or are still working for corporations. They may have a desire to have control over their own destiny and may want a more heartfelt life. I know lots of people who made a choice to move out on their own.

Money Stories

Those who stay in corporations find a way to make it work. They may stay because they have family situations that won't allow them to go out on their own. I think those people are probably right where they need to be.

A company is only as good as its people. As for me, being self-employed is a spiritual practice. It requires faith every single day in so many ways. I get to decide who I will and won't work with. Every decision, every choice, is an opportunity to look at ourselves and understand why we do what we do or why I do what I do. I love being able to put my life together the way I want to put it together. If I make wrong choices, well, the buck stops here, as they say.

For a long time I thought that if you were on the right path, the money would come to you no matter what. If you are here to be a writer, then the money would come to you and you wouldn't have to work at another job. But I've seen lots of examples where this doesn't happen. In one of Oriah Mt. Dreamer's books, she says that very few writers, artists, and other creative people can just do their creative work. Most must have a job along with their art. Are most of your clients or students doing their creative work along with another job?

Most of my one-on-one clients do not have another job. Their work, their message, is their livelihood. They have found a way to make it work through their books, speaking, consulting, and other kinds of trainings and programs. They've also done that inner work that I mentioned replacing any negative messages about who they are, or how bad it is to make money, or whatever, to something much more positive that propels them toward their goals.

Many who are in my classes, both virtual and on the ground, are still learning and so they may have

Knowing What You Want

a job, but they have a dream of supporting themselves and their families with their purpose work. They are actively working toward that and it's incredible to witness them change. They set goals and timelines to get out of their job and devote their time and life toward reaching their dream.

But you are so right; no matter the situation, it still takes work. You can have this dream and this passion and this talent and this yearning and you're trying to make something happen. You are still going to have to do the work to take your message out into the world.

It is a myth to think that it will flow all the time. It reminds me of Suzanne Falter Barnes, who has been a client of mine for years. She wrote a book called *How Much Joy Can You Stand?* She said "Even when you are working on your dream, there are times when it still sucks."

"Here" is what you need to remember when you are having a hard time. And that "here" is life, by the way. Even when you're doing something you love, there are aspects you won't love, and that's just life. It is a fantasy to think you're going to love all aspects of anything, all the time. You can be in the best relationship in the world and there are things you are just not going to like about the relationship or your partner, and that's just how it is. That doesn't mean it isn't the right relationship, or you're in the wrong line of work, or your dream just isn't really it.

I believe maturity is learning how to deal with the things that aren't so much fun. I mean, really, who loves running to their desk to get those taxes done? Or facing the blank page when it's time to get a writing project done, or facing some life crisis? Getting past those difficult tasks and enjoying the things you do love

Money Stories

is what needs to happen. How many people love to get out and exercise? You know it's good for you. Thank goodness for the endorphins that get stirred up or I don't know who would do it. You're never going to find something that you love all the time, and if you think you can, you'll probably be disappointed. It gets easier if you focus on the aspects you do love. Do the other things, but don't get all hung up in how much you don't like them. It's simply a part of life.

Here's another example: I don't like billing. I don't like it at all. It's not what I want to do. I went through a stage where I thought I could learn to love it. But that didn't happen. As you become more successful in what you do, you can hire someone to do that kind of work for you. As you grow and expand, you eventually get to the place where someone else can take it over, and that's a wonderful place to be.

Then you have to make the decision. "Do I want to be bigger than my business is now or not?"

It's funny, in fact. I've had people tell me that I could add this and do that and have employees. I've had employees and didn't like it. Suddenly, I had to manage people rather than doing the work I loved, and at that point I realized I don't want to build an empire. What I have right now works for me. There are other things I want to do. I certainly have dreams in areas I want to explore. But it has never been about bigger, better, more, more, more for me. This works for me. What I have now makes me happy. I'm meeting wonderful people. I feel really blessed and lucky.

The lovely thing is that most people I've worked with stay in touch. They come to a workshop or virtually through a webinar or teleseminar; they learn how to get media attention, how to promote their businesses,

Knowing What You Want

how to do social media effectively, etc. Many of them have gone forward and have gotten articles in various magazines and newspapers or are interviewed on radio and television or are creating their own video content.

One woman who came to a workshop is now a regular doing a morning TV show. She came to my webinar class and was ready. Taking my program gave her the fundamentals and lots of confidence to move forward. The workshop gave her an extra little boost. Many others come to me virtually, now, and they are all over the world. It is very satisfying, especially since we've built this wonderful, supportive community. They get a lot out of it, and I certainly get a great deal from it.

It really depends on how ready someone is. Some people come to a webinar or they take one of my programs out of curiosity and realize that they need to do other things before they can use the information, like clearing out old messages from childhood or setting up some marketing, getting their product in stores or getting a catalog. Then they can start the publicity push. Sometimes the webinar or workshop just points out what they need to do first.

Did you have to clear out stuff when you first started your business? Is that how you knew about this part of the process?

Listen, I've been in the trenches! I remember when I started out, I had a client who really wanted to be on a morning news show like Today or Good Morning America, and I'd send her materials to those shows. Then I'd need to call the producers. I remember I had to walk around the house, like ten times, getting up the nerve to call and pitch them. I found that the only way out is through. You make enough calls, you get better at it, and it gets easier.

Money Stories

You know agreement number two of Don Miguel Ruiz's Four Agreements about not taking things personally? That is at the top of the list. It's not about you. If you can learn that, 90% is done. Funny how that happens.

Initially, when you are starting out, you have to be kind to yourself. Pat yourself on the back just because you went ahead and took the steps and tried. Who else is going to do that for you if you don't do it for yourself? It's so important at the beginning. Then, you get better at putting yourself out there.

Also, if there is a day when you don't feel like you can connect with people on the phone, do something else. Do some writing or clean the office. I'm not saying you should make calls only when you feel like it. That's like saying write only when you feel like it. I don't believe that either. I think you've got to set a time and do it, and there are always distractions. I also think we know when we're procrastinating, so get clear on when you need to take a day off from trying to connect with people because you need it, and when you are procrastinating because you don't want to do it. There's a huge difference.

I understand. You've got to get into a rhythm and push through. But there are some days that you would push people away rather than draw them in. Do you find that once you are in your power and doing what you came here to do that money comes easier?

Yes. There are tools you can use to help you get in the right frame of mind when you are working on your business or your craft. Before reaching out to people, it's good to ask yourself some important questions. Many people use affirmations, but I find questions to be more powerful because your brain always comes up

Knowing What You Want

with answers. For example, when you're getting ready to do some outreach, ask yourself, "How dynamic am I going to be today?" or, "How come people love to say 'yes' to me?" or "How much fun am I going to have connecting with people today." Ask the question, and then most importantly, listen for the answer. "How dynamic am I going to be today" presupposes that you are going to be dynamic. This is very powerful stuff. Before you do the outreach, you must be in the right state emotionally. That is the biggest key. When others sense you are congruent and care about them, business and money come more easily.

My advice when you do this outreach is to take the focus off yourself and put it on the other person. How can you help them? If you can do that and you truly want to help them, without your own stuff getting in the way, you've got it. We all have to pay the mortgage and take care of those financial things and we need to trust the universe.

When you are talking to people, the conversation needs to be about taking the focus off you and putting it on them. What will help them solve their problems? Another thing to keep in mind is that maybe the money isn't going to come from them. Maybe they are not going to be the ones to buy your product or service, but because you spoke with them, it now is going to come from some other source that is tapped because you talked with them. I've seen it happen lots of times. I believe you have to give, give, give and equally you have to receive, receive, receive.

I know that when you open yourself up, you don't get to pick which channels open up.

That doesn't mean don't open yourself up. When I was in radio broadcasting, I used to go on auditions for commercials. I had an agent who sent me to all these auditions and I never got anything through that agent. I got work on my own. Of course, I still had to pay the agent. Does that mean it was worthless to pay the agent? I don't think so. You do the work, you do what's in front of you, and see the doors open. That's an example from my life.

Was it worth it to have an agent or did the agent provide other benefits?

I met a lot of people and the experience of interviews was great. Eventually, we did part ways because I was managing on my own, but it was a good learning experience. It's about taking the best out of any experience, learning from it, and making decisions to stay in the situation or move to something else.

So have you gotten clients from your webinars and programs?

Oh yes. Sometimes people take my visibility program or my publicity and marketing program and they start doing their own publicity only to realize it's a lot of work. They have to make the decision to either continue or hire someone to do it. I have the good fortune of having some people deciding that they want to do other things, so they hire me. There's an awful lot to this. It isn't brain surgery, but it takes persistence, curiosity, a willingness to put yourself out there, and there are a lot of details.

I tell people to stand in their power. Knowing what you want is so critical in having a vision. If you focus on how you can give and help others instead of falling into your fear, step by step, day by day, you will accomplish what you want. You will get there!

Knowing What You Want

Things to think about:
Are you able to manifest what you need in your life? Here's a meditation from Joanne that might help you focus your energy and manifest.

Turn off your phone and other demanding technology. Find a comfortable place to sit. Close your eyes. Take three deep breaths. As you let out each breath, watch for tight or tense places in your body. Imagine your breathe going to those places to help you relax.

Now imagine yourself at 98 and ask your 98-year-old self to go for a walk with you. Imagine that you have walked to a place that is comfortable and safe and pleasing to you both. Ask your 98-year-old self to ask you how you are doing now. Just listen to what comes into your mind. After a minute or so imagine the questions you'd like to ask, such as, "What can I do to manifest what I need or want in my life?" Just listen and *do not judge* what words or thoughts come to mind. If you don't receive any answers, just allow yourself to be comfortable and quiet. Maybe your answer is that you have what you need at this time or that it's not time for changes yet.

Sometimes we disregard the first, very quiet message that comes, so listen carefully to the first thought that comes to mind. Is that your message? Just keep doing this exercise and trusting and you will begin to get answers that will help you.

After a few minutes thank your 98-year-old self for being with you and imagine the two of you walking back to where you began. Write down the insights you received on your journey. Don't forget to thank any spirit guides that came along to help.

Money Stories

I first heard about **Peace Pilgrim** in a staff meetings at New Renaissance Bookshop. At these meetings, buyers would bring new product to share so staff could be knowledgeable. Karin LaBriere, the video buyer, brought a group of new videos for us to sample. The documentary about Peace Pilgrim, a woman in her 50s who gave up money and began walking for peace, was the first one she showed us and none of us wanted it to stop. I was totally drawn to Peace Pilgrim's way of moving toward her mission.

     Since that first "meeting" about 13 years ago, I have been drawn to Peace Pilgrim and feel that she has become my guru of sorts. Though I don't see myself giving up on money, her messages of trust and faith have become my guiding principles. I knew I had to include her story, even though her path didn't include money and I could not interview her since she died in the early 1980s. The following is an excerpt and paraphrase of portions of her memoir.

Chapter 18

Pilgrimage for Peace

"I walk until given shelter, fast until given food. I don't ask – it's given without asking. Aren't people good! There is a spark of good in everybody, no matter how deeply it may be buried, it is there." Peace Pilgrim

From 1953 to 1981, silver-haired Mildred Lisette Norman, calling herself only "Peace Pilgrim," walked on a personal pilgrimage for peace. She vowed to "remain a wanderer until mankind has learned the way of peace, walking until given shelter and fasting until given food." During these 28 years and way over 25,000 miles, she touched the hearts, minds, and lives of thousands of individuals across North America. Her message continues to inspire people around the world.

Peace Pilgrim's story tells how she lived her last three decades without money or possessions. This is not a journey that most of us would tackle, but it's a fascinating choice and an interesting lesson in trust.

I was drawn to Peace Pilgrim's story the moment I heard about her, which was about 15 years after her death. My friend Sharlene Inglis, had even met Peace Pilgrim when she gave a talk at Sharlene's church.

Money Stories

My first question was why would anyone make a choice like this? The next question was how did she learn that level of trust? Peace Pilgrim didn't begin to walk because of money problems. She began because she was drawn to a path that would make a difference.

Her story really begins in 1952 on an early morning walk when she says she attained inner peace. "All of a sudden I felt very uplifted, more uplifted than I had ever been. I remember I knew timelessness and spacelessness and lightness. I did not seem to be walking on the earth. There were no people or even animals around, but every flower, every bush, every tree seemed to wear a halo. There was a light emanation around everything and flecks of gold fell like slanted rain through the air.

"The most important part of it was not the phenomena: the important part of it was the realization of the oneness of all creation. Not only all human beings – I knew before that all human beings are one. But now I knew also a oneness with the rest of creation. The creatures that walk the earth and the growing things of the earth. The air, the water, the earth itself. And, most wonderful of all, a oneness with that which permeates all and binds all together and gives life to all. A oneness with that which many would call God."

"I have never felt separate since. I could return again and again to this wonderful mountaintop, and then I could stay there for longer and longer periods of time and just slip out occasionally."

It was at this time that the inspiration for her pilgrimage came. First, she asked God to help her remain in harmony, because every time she slipped out of harmony, it impaired her usefulness. During this time she was drawn toward the idea of a pilgrimage, which she felt was a special way of witnessing for peace.

Pilgrimage for Peace

"I saw, in my mind's eye, myself walking along and wearing the garb of my mission... I saw a map of the United States with the large cities marked – and it was as though someone had taken a colored crayon and marked a zigzag line across, coast to coast and border to border, from Los Angeles to New York City. I knew what I was to do. And that was a vision of my first year's pilgrimage route in 1953!"

Her life all of a sudden had purpose and meaning.

Mildred's pilgrimage began on New Years Day in 1953 at the Tournament of Roses parade in Pasadena, California. She walked ahead of the parade, talking to people and handing out peace messages. Peace Pilgrim was surprised to see a genuine interest in peace, but about halfway along the route a policeman stopped her. Though she was sure he was going to eject her from the parade, instead, he told her he thought thousands more like her were needed!

Peace Pilgrim wore a simple dark sleeveless tunic, with pockets to carry her few possessions. When she left Pasadena, the tunic read PEACE PILGRIM on the front and Walking Coast to Coast for Peace on the back. Over the years the back's message changed from Walking 10,000 Miles for World Disarmament to Walking 25,000 Miles for Peace and ending with the message 25,000 Miles on Foot for Peace. Her walk took her several times into the continental 48 states, as well as Mexico and all ten Canadian provinces.

Peace Pilgrim counted miles from the beginning of 1953 to the fall of 1964 when she arrived in Washington, D.C. At that point she decided to stop counting. "25,000 miles is enough." Counting had tied her to main highways where mileage was on maps. But highways

Money Stories

were not good places to meet people. "Now I'm free to walk where people are."

At the beginning of her pilgrimage, she only walked and would not take rides. In her memoir Peace Pilgrim tells several stories about this choice.

"It was my experience of walking through a dust storm which sometimes blew with such force I could scarcely stand against it, while sometimes the dust was so thick I could not see ahead and could only guide myself by the edge of the road. A policeman stopped alongside me, threw open his car door and yelled, "Get in here, woman, before you get killed." I told him I was walking a pilgrimage and did not accept rides (at that time). I also told him that God was my shield and there was nothing to fear. At that moment the winds died down, the dust settled and the sun broke from the clouds. I continued to walk. But the wonderful thing was that I felt spiritually lifted above the hardship.

"On my pilgrimage a lot of cars stopped and people invited me to ride. Some thought walking meant hitchhiking. I told them I did not cheat God – you don't cheat about counting miles on a pilgrimage."

Here's another story: "One test happened in the middle of the night in the middle of the California desert. The traffic had just about stopped, and there wasn't a human habitation within many miles. I saw a car parked at the side of the road. The driver called to me saying, 'Come on, get in and get warm.' I said, 'I don't ride.'

"He said, 'I'm not going anywhere, I'm just parked here.' I got in. I looked at the man. He was a big, burly man – what most people would call a rough looking individual. After we had talked a while he said, 'Say, wouldn't you like to get a few winks of sleep?' And

Pilgrimage for Peace

I said, 'Oh, yes, I certainly would!' And I curled up and went to sleep. When I awoke, I could see the man was very puzzled about something, and after we had talked for quite some time he admitted that when he had asked me to get into the car, he had certainly meant me no good, adding, 'When you curled up so trustingly and went to sleep, I just couldn't touch you!'"

"I thanked him for the shelter and began walking away. As I looked back, I saw him gazing at the heavens, and I hoped he had found God that night."

On her journey Peace Pilgrim made the decision to "walk until given shelter, fast until given food." In her memoir, she tells about the difficulties of this decision. "Some things don't seem so difficult, like going without food. I seldom miss more than three to four meals in a row and I never even think about food until it is offered. The most I have gone without food is three days, and then mother nature provided my food – apples that had fallen from a tree. I once fasted as a prayer discipline for 45 days, so I know how long one can go without food! My problem is not how to get enough to eat; it's how to graciously avoid getting too much. Everyone wants to overfeed me!

"Going without sleep would be harder, although I can miss one night's sleep and I don't mind. Every once in awhile I miss a night's sleep, but not for some time now. The last time was September of 1977 when I was in a truck stop. I had intended to sleep a little but it was such a busy truck stop that I spent all night talking to truck drivers. The first thing after I went in, a truck driver who'd seen me on television wanted to buy me some food. I sat in a corner booth. Then truck drivers started to arrive, and it was just one wave of truck drivers after another that were standing there and asking

Money Stories

me questions, and so forth. I actually talked to them all night and I never did get to do any sleeping. After awhile somebody offered me breakfast and I ate that and left."

"I can say to my body, 'Lie down there on that cement floor and go to sleep,' and it obeys. I can say to my mind, 'Shut out everything else and concentrate on the job before you,' and it is obedient. I can say to my emotions, 'Be still, even in the face of this terrible situation,' and they are still. A great philosopher has said he who seems to be out of step may be following a different drummer."

Peace Pilgrim realized her "calling" in 1952 during the Korean War and the McCarthy era. She says that it was a time of fear and for most people it was safest to be apathetic. "Yes, it was most certainly a time for a pilgrim to step forward, because a pilgrim's job is to rouse people from apathy and make them think.

"...A pilgrimage can be to a place – that's the best known kind – but it can also be for a thing. Mine is for peace, and that is why I am a Peace Pilgrim."

"My pilgrimage covers the entire peace picture: peace among nations, peace among groups, peace within our environment, peace among individuals, and the very, very important inner peace – which I talk about most often because that is where peace begins."

"The situation in the world around us is just a reflection of the collective situation. In the final analysis, only as we become more peaceful people will we be finding ourselves living in a more peaceful world."

"In the Middle Ages the pilgrims went out as the disciples were sent out – without money, without food, without adequate clothing – and I know that tradition. I have no money. I do not accept any money on my pil-

Pilgrimage for Peace

grimage. I belong to no organization. There is no organization backing me. I own only what I wear and carry. There is nothing to tie me down. I am as free as a bird soaring in the sky."

"I walk until given shelter, fast until given food. I don't ask – it's given without asking. Aren't people good! There is a spark of good in everybody, no matter how deeply it may be buried, it is there. It's waiting to govern your life gloriously."

Peace Pilgrim's stories "on the road" are many and she still inspires me, even 13 years after first hearing about her.

You can read the entire memoir *The Peace Pilgrim, Her Life and Her Work In Her Own Words* on the web at peacepilgrim.com. Her book is also available from New Renaissance Bookshop, www.newrenbooks.com.

Things to think about:

Peace Pilgrim's mission was to walk for peace and she did that for 28 years. What would your mission or pilgrimage look like? Would you stop doing anything or step out to take on some world, national, local, or personal issue?

Peace Pilgrim's journey was for peace. Mine is about trust that I'm following the right path and about listening. Do you know what your life's mission is? If you were to follow your mission, would you be doing something different than you are now? What would it take for you to follow the path of your life's mission? If you had to make changes in order to follow your mission, what would those changes look like? If your life would stay as it is, congratulations to you!

Closing

I started this book as a personal journey to find answers about money, and each chapter has brought me amazing insights, though not necessarily what I thought I'd find. And the insights seems to change each time I read a chapter. Your insights will probably be totally different from mine, and that's great.

So what have I learned?

Insight 1 – Trust

Insight 1 is about trust. Trust is my major lifetime lesson. Most of my life I've been a big worrier and struggler, but I've realized in the course of this project that all of my worry comes from not trusting and not wanting to turn my life over to Spirit/God. My astrology says I have problems with authority. That even rolls over into my spiritual life, and the questions are who's in charge and how to stand in my power AND turn my life over to Spirit/God.

Aren't being in your power and being in control synonymous? No, not to me. The way I define standing in my power is not being a victim of what's happening, finding my way in spite of what's going on around me. Letting go of control has to do with listening to my intuition about what I need to do and what's my next step, not being stuck with a plan that is etched in cement and doesn't allow for change and flexibility.

Money Stories

Trust, to me, is about listening to that still small voice inside me or the voice that comes through pulling a card from one of my inspirational decks. Trust may also be about making a move because I know I need to make it even though it doesn't seem logical.

I've always found that when I trust and follow Spirit's guidance, I'm supported. Maybe not in the way I had envisioned or wanted, but the support is there.

Insight 2 – More versus Enough

This insight is about more versus enough, and my story around these. For over half of my life my story was that I needed "more" to be okay: more money, more things, more time, more happiness, more of everything. Enough was not a concept I understood. I saw the struggles I was having and what I didn't have, not what I did have.

A gift from this book is about gratitude. I'm amazed at how much I've had and not been grateful for. Replacing needing/wanting more with gratitude has changed my personal story from "don't have" to knowing I'll be supported. I've learned that fulfillment comes from "enough, not more." We don't gain access to anything by wanting and needing "more" because in that position we are always striving for that "more." I've found that I needed to change my focus to see the blessing of enough and to have gratitude for that. Seeing that I have enough and having gratitude are now my daily practice.

I can always think of something more I need or want, but focusing on what I have and being thankful entirely changes my energy. Now I see and am grateful for clients and students who paid me to teach them and they, in turn, helped me learn what I needed to learn next. I'm also grateful for my home of eleven years and

Closing

the job that gave me the opportunity to meet many of the interesting people in this book. Changing my focus was and is a very important part of allowing "enough" to be my story. I'm happy and doing what I want to do, rather than being needy and a victim of what is happening around me.

Insight 3 – Values

Third, I've learned about values. I used to focus so much on having more money that I didn't realize that creativity and freedom are what I really long for. I thought that having money was the top value because I always needed more than I had. But though I enjoy and love having money, it's not at the top of my list. Working with this book I remembered many years ago taking a values test and finding that freedom is my top value and creativity comes up close behind. Money is about fifth on that list of what I value. I need to be doing things that allow me to feel fulfilled, creative, and free when I am making my money. As Lewis Mehl-Madrona said, "Whenever I've done something just for the money it has always been a really bad idea." That is true for me as well.

I've done a lot of things to bring in money but for the most part I've been totally ignorant of how those jobs fit with my values. I'm not sure if my life would have been easier or different if I had looked at how my values fit a particular job, but I'm glad that my last job and the work I'm doing now, including this book, fit those values. Thank you, Spirit.

Insight 4 – Action

The fourth insight is the need for action after I've identified what is important and of value and part of my story. It's easy to wish for something, but to achieve that

Money Stories

something usually takes action. That is the point of Lori Wilson's chapter, that once you have the education, you need to move out and take the necessary steps to build your business and invite in the resources that are necessary to keep your work going. It's difficult to step out and speak or act on your truth, but that is what we are ultimately here for. If you are here to be a medical intuitive and don't take the steps to get your shingle out there, think of the people you were supposed to help who won't get the benefit of your wisdom and insights. It may be difficult to step out there, but once you take those first steps you may be surprised how powerful you feel. This is right livelihood and following your path.

Things to think about:
Do you know what your lessons are for this lifetime? Are you working on trust or balance or responsibility or control or acceptance or something else? How do those lessons affect your life path and your struggles? Can you easily let go and allow change to happen or do you try to keep your life tightly controlled no matter what? If you are a tight controller, how do you feel about how your life is unfolding? If you tend toward more flexibility, how does that affect your life? What insights have you learned about your story?

I have learned that I can and do want to have tight control over my life and what happens, but that my life runs better if I can open up my arms and give control to Spirit/God. At times when I am not able to let go of control, I suffer and struggle more. As soon as I am able to surrender, I find that I feel better and my life usually settles down and becomes more comfortable. Good luck finding your best way.

About Connie:
Connie Carmichael Hill moved to Oregon in 1969 and even loves the area's rain. She raised two daughters alone, and after being laid off from a large electronics company, found her passion at Portland's New Renaissance Bookshop. At the book store she spent 12 years coordinating events with spiritual authors and teachers. While at the book store she had the pleasure of meeting and exercising her "nosey-bone," interviewing 45 well-known spiritual teachers for a local alternative newspaper. Connie has also helped hundreds make drums and rattles, and lots of others make personal changes with astrology. Contact Connie at gmknite@gmail.com

Money Stories

Notes

Money Stories

Notes

Money Stories

Notes

Money Stories

www.ingramcontent.com/pod-product-compliance
Lightning Source LLC
Chambersburg PA
CBHW051753040426
42446CB00007B/350